CheapGestures
Writings

Poems
Essays
Meditations
Translations

Bill Davis

Fomite
Burlington, VT

Copyright 2025 © Bill Davis
Cover image 2025 © Bill Davis

All rights reserved. No part of this book may be reproduced in any form or by any means without the prior written consent, except in the case of brief quotations used in reviews and certain other noncommercial uses permitted by copyright law. This is a work of fiction. Any resemblance between the characters of these stories and real people, living or dead, is merely coincidental.

ISBN-13: 978-1-947917-48-4
Library of Congress Control Number: 2023947780
Fomite
58 Peru Street
Burlington, VT 05401
03/12/2025

*Dedicated to Maxine Blanchard,
Renata Davis and Wes Davis*

Contents

Poems 1975-1982

War Notebooks	5
Four Afterthoughts	10
A Partial Geography	12
Gardens	18
Endless Shape & a Single Effect	19
If There Are Cameras	20
Sailing to the New World	21
Anamnesis	22
No Vacancy (Invoking the Motels)	23
Untitled	24

from *Local 254* 1976

The Gates	27
The Union Man	28
White Shoes	29
Ballplayers	30
Joe Mooney	32
An Address by Vice-President Aleviszos Before a Game with the Milwaukee Brewers in June 1973 in Section 33 in Left Field	34
Fourteen Dollars and Forty-Five Cents	37
Why People Watch Baseball	39

Sweet Framingham Cadenzas

Sweet Framingham Cadenzas Nos. 1-33	43

Poems 1977

Paradise	61
Angelina at Twilight	63
Reflection	65
Radios on the Beach	66
In the arms of my dreams there were horses	67
Footfalls	68
Blue Plume Midnights	69

Waiting Room: A Numbered, Alphabetical Inventory	71
Marjorie's Favorites	73
I Am Not So Sure I Am Not So Sure	75

from *Separations* 1977

Equidistances	79
Intersections	91

Cheap Gestures

Side 1
    1. Nurses Instructions 105
    2. No One Forced Karl Marx 106
    3. Jaccottet Dub   107
Side 2
    Last Laugh   108

Three Days Later

First Blurts	113
2 Songs Orpheus Got Wrong	115
Phase Locked Loop	117
Van Gogh Hangs on Pushpins Like a Windmill on a Vast Plain	118
Three Days Later	120
rooms	121

from *Boys Will Be Boys*

Phrase Book	129
My Advice Is	130
One of Those Modern Angels	131
Trading a Blind Horse (Part 2)	132
Parallel	134

Translations

Francis Ponge

La Barque	139
Le Magnolia	140
The Cigarette	141

Gérard de Nerval from *Les Chimères*
    Naming Her   145
    A Madame Aguado   152
    El Desdichado   153
    Myrtho   154
    Delfica   155
    Horus   156
    Vers Dores   157
    Artemis   158

from *You Can See That It's Just The Walls That Are Standing (Just Empty Walls)*
    Photos Small, 3 inches by 1 1/2 inches   161
    Photograph Number 182   165
    Photographs: Silvery, Angular Tabs   171
    July 29, 1945 In the Philippines Rec'd August 6, 1945   179
    October 21, 1945 Leyte   183
    "Billy"   185
    4 Photographs   189
    Colorado, 1954   193
    Photograph: Small Leather Folder   196
    Smooth, round, fountain-pen   201

Essay on 9/11   203

made again a firmament   219

I wanted/to tell /to ask   225

The Coach Road Landscapes   241

Introduction

Bill Davis was born in Queens, New York in 1949. In 1975, he moved to Burlington, Vermont, where he has remained. Over the thirty or so years that he wrote the poems, essays, translations, and prose pieces in this book, he managed a cooperative bookstore, freelanced as a sportswriter, worked at two colleges as an IT specialist, and researched and produced an online journal for mental health professionals. He also composed and performed electronic music, often collaborating with dancers and choreographers.

But these bits of biography only glance the many surfaces and interiors of his writing. It's not so easy to characterize, that voice: sometimes sardonic; sometimes drilled into granular detail; sometimes verging on synesthesia, sometimes extremely tender; often playful, colloquial, and cerebral at the same time. Culture, what humans have made in and of the world, is his playground, as language, with all its mysterious contradiction, is his medium.

Bill found an unusual and lively group of writers in Burlington in the mid-1970's, already producing little magazines, chapbooks, tracts, broadsides, and other alternatives to traditional and academic publishing, starting with a mimeograph machine. Poets' Mimeo, as it was called for a while, also convened regular readings in various free spaces around town. Much of Bill's work was published in this way, and we have followed that chronology and those groupings as we assembled his work for this collection.

In August of 2005, Bill suffered a massive stroke, which left him with severe global aphasia. As he healed, he gradually recovered the ability to read and to understand speech, as well as to navigate the riches of the Internet with his computer. But the writing was over. Instead, he publishes several blogs -- Deep Art Nature, Scissors Kick, and 1960's: Days of Rage--sharing his discoveries about popular culture, cities, maps, painting, performance, radical politics, sports (mostly soccer and baseball), movies, dance, music, and much more.

Anna Blackmer
Michael Breiner
Co-Editors

Poems
1975-1982

War Notebooks

1 / mayday   1975
in the final weeks the rumors were fantastic
at the formica counters of the Café Givral
on the outskirts of the city: nipping at espresso
waiting for the boy with the newspapers
who may know about a coup in Hanoi
or an imaginary assault at Truong Div
who may bring a letter from an imaginary friend
which could still be exchanged for a visa
with the present authorities

I was drinking coffee & reading the Globe
that morning   listening to the radio in the kitchen
looking at the clock over the cash register
waiting for your bus to arrive
as scallop boats drifted into the harbor

it was spring
there was fresh rain on the sweetflag & the stargrass
the sun brilliant on the blue surface of the waters
everything exploding with spores & seeds
the April sea certain and cold
& Saigon had finally fallen during the night

2
tonight I watch you
undressing in the moonlight

we were innocent of our own power
for so long it seems

until the wounds opened again
until we learned it could still be used
how it gathers and grows invisibly
in the blind current
roaring below the surface
where there is no protection
and everything has hooks

you stand there
with your eyes down
and I see how afraid you are

I want to say yes I understand
I want to pretend we can comfort each other
like wounded sexless things of the atmosphere
trapped in a basement during the siege
repairing our wings & our voices
waiting out the night
and O sister
I am afraid too
even if I speak the same language

3 / "the will to change begins in the body" -Adrienne Rich

if the will to change begins in the body
it begins in the unprotected core
untouched by this force I feel
which is not me
but inhabits me
shaping itself into a fist
beating the mattress desperately
like an involuntary spasm of flame

flickering in the dark liquid
breathing smoke into the vacuum of the cells
exploding suddenly without warning
radiating from my skin
like the smell of a killer
and the incandescent glow
of fused filaments
as the surge comes up from nowhere

4 / photographs

a man is trying to hang from the landing gear
of a transport leaving for the tent-camps on Guam

two soldiers are standing in the doorway
and the children are watching them

a woman is waving a telegram from her American lover
while others in front of her are trying to push
past the police guarding the Embassy gates

a helicopter ascends   lurching from the crowded roof
like a bloated insect beating its thin metal wings
climbing up through the smoke

5
there is an unopened universe
an uncharted region of vast dimension
smooth as the sheets in winter
like the blank imagined interior

on early maps of the continent
before it was completely subdued

I am a man yes   but I am waiting for the end
lying here with you
praying for the fall of the kingdoms
& hoping to be done at last with this way of speaking
to be rid of these useless things
to begin again gently
to begin again
yes
gently this time

there is no desire now   no passion
nothing is finished yet
there are no necessities now
no dreams & no plans & no memories
it is a question of being conscious
now and simple acts of compassion

6
tonight we are crowded together in your bed
with two children who have been evicted
it is two in the morning
and we talk quietly
over their deep breathing
and the drone of airplanes
over the city
slipping into sleep
not willing to touch or wound
or fail or compromise any longer
brushing the cheek of one of the children

I dream we are all together in the vanguard
of an evolutionary strain
in which everything dead & violent
has been overthrown & transformed
and it is possible not
to reconstruct the body
rising out of the ash on wings

the last flag has been torn down
from the last hamlet
the land is being tilled
small boats move up the delta
the moon rises over the bay
and we are running up the wet streets
dancing with all our sisters & brothers
as an ambulance sings through the night.

1975

Four Afterthoughts
for Susan Brown

We are forgiven our dreams
aren't we?
This is the last lesson
in dismantling the props,
the romantic atmosphere.
There is in fact only action.
We never did make it to the park.
We told stories, dropped spoons,
& threw stones into the whitecaps
until the dogs cried.
*

But I found it all again:
birds in flight, the sun purpled
on the cold plate of the mind
& minute correspondences
of year to year, day by day,
step by step through the pale vine-gardens,
silver shining where you were lying
& the grass is still
remembering. You smell
like the beekeeper's daughter
you are.
*

Clover shoots are choking on the stinkweed,
foam dripping from the tulips' undersides
& as your tongue is touching
only the edges of my teeth,
roses are burning up
out of the blizzards
into the air, the afterlife
of the skin's memories of hell.

*

You are eating figs.
I am eating my words.
We are figments of the real
trying to translate an original feeling
into the language's present tense,
the syntax of our sentences
taut in the body's instincts,
the incoherent brushwork
on the wings of its prehistory.
A prisoner's lament
floats across a courtyard in New Jersey.
My presentiments
exactly.

1977

A Partial Geography

1. Into the shape of the road the road goes.
   It is a farm.
   It is stitched.
   No, it has flowers.
   It has time to reconstruct.

   The water is waiting.

   In the summer comes a blue chamber, a bounded blue, a stir
   that has a shape on the surface like a French explorer, or
   a forest, a first name.

2. Absorbing a bow.
   Bending in cages.
   Cleaning a door.

3. I set the silverware myself. A spoon beside a fork on the
   colored napkin and with my fingers to cradle the folds
   before the skin slips.
   It is silver.
   I empty the glass when I make my lips stretch.

4. Out of the circle comes a line, and this all has a hesitation
   to waste.
   We make songs.
   We make a shade exact & tactile and we never were satisfied.

   Out of the circle comes a line and in the summer it was
   talkative, in the dinners, cylindrical, the sound of the
   glasses, in passing.
   It was silver in the morning.
   It was blue six hours at a time.

Out of the circle comes a line and in the summer it rinses clean.
Breathing.
A gray chair in the distance a breath is: a word, not a world it has to be scrambled in.
To be broken.
To be changing.
To be one word longer and not to be tame.

5. Dying. Enfolding.
   Exacting a float.
   Flickering.
   A garden, a guardrail.
   Himself.

6. The chain is not rivers.
   It is not a chain of haste.
   Its displacement.
   Skeletons on a scale mirrored (impossible) with fish, and with white caps on the little ones hand in hand.

7. Hemisphere.
   An Image. Inert.

8. If inching is helpful the digging is green and particularly not a blue but moving forward, leaf by leaf on a darkness sometimes knotted.
   A night.
   Not opening.

   Wisdom is a pale and sometimes a flush of privilege in a broad path, but not to be victimized if the inching is raw or real.

"Never try to arrange things," the text says. "Things and poems are irreconcilable."

9. A space centered before it could rise.
   A cedar the eyes are refusing.
   A sail.
   And sometimes in the east.

10. In sufficient juggling.
    Knuckles and a lens.
    Loosening a mainspring not an oar.
    Maybe: negative, or "one to be subtracted."

11. Over the water a sleep lies, a slave, in the course of a certain solstice, that is: a white hand lifts a red fruit.
    The darkening is permitted and the patience is cool.
    The jeweled spaces can fit in the silk-tight whiskey, the unused postcards, the suns sleeping on nails.

12. The pails were heavy and the water was Scandinavian as their voices came through the various trees and on the stones then the pouring water into the ground.
    Cedar ash oak and columbine.
    The ground is tight and the daughters were not Scandinavian.
    Or the noises white.
    Or geese on the bones.
    Or sisters.
    With buckets.
    With haste.

13. Gunshots I whispered.

14. Optative projectors.

A portable quest, no: a question.
A quick and reciprocal science.

15. To begin with bracelets.
    To begin with singing.
    Not to betray or to be afraid, the honey locked so loosely
      in the pockets.

    How harmony happens cannot be predicted without harm.
    Starts and stops the individual stops and starts.
    If she played any softer she wouldn't be playing.

16. Radios and a gunmetal shoreline I filter through and to when
      the shape of the melody is yours.
    It is "Becalmed," or "Little Fishes" or "Pills" or "Trash" or
    "Chatterbox" or "The Girls Want To Be With the Girls."
    A hookless monotone in a practiced zone of accessories to be
    flattened out in waves: a wind, and a war, and a blind
    compression.

    Four folds of plum overlaying a simple green and a contour
      if that.
    We figured the playlist at sixty in one-and-a half-hour shots.

17. One indication of arriving was a little more motion not stopping,
      so the promise was intermittently its own deliverance, and
      always the same.
    There the air goes and there it doesn't.
    A flower can be on a sleeve if it is.
    A poem can be peculiar.
    It has names for colors, it imagines itself a barrier.
    It sucks and spits.
    A lamp is another example.

18. A raiment is a smooth and a tight utensil.
    She trims under velvet with a whisper, an x-ray, yes,
      yours truly, a zone of alphabets.

19. Ozone so close it was empty in the lightning.
    The smell was not arms, it was not our ribs, it was not a
      permission.

    I think what we could see.
    I think we were not looking at the time.
    Here I have time to reconstruct.

    Does this mean stopping?
    No it means not to be disappointed.

20. An island is not a silence.
    The motion is not an equivalence.
    The division is continuous.
    I lift and I lower in one motion, mistaking a motorboat for
      the rain.
    A word not the world enclosed in other words where a wind blows
      through them and out.
    A door. A candle. A matchbook. A key. A screen. A ranging. A
      kitchen light. A cross. A shore. A scent.

21. Why is she walking there.
    That motorboat.
    That day.

22. I sift and I sew what is learning.
    I light a lamp.
    She walks.
    She whistles.
    I stand.

I am older, doubling back.
I set the silverware myself.
A spoon beside a fork on the colored napkin and with my
 fingers to cradle the folds before the skin slips.
Into the shape of the road.

Gardens

there is a white landscape
where the birds are waiting
where the sweetbriar & pennycress
hold round whole droplets of blue

once the thief
the predator
returning as a servant now
to the gardens of the nebula
in the web
in the dew
in the shimmering

1976

Endless Shape & a Single Effect

This is a darkened room
in a house of light.
I practice
lifting the cup
quietly. Re-
placing it.
I try to place a cup
exactly in the middle of a poem
but the words don't come
with effort.
They can barely
remember for example
how I was moving exactly
where the lamp was on the table.
Your legs in New York
taut & white
walking on tiptoe
overlooking a stone garden
from barred windows
& brushing the ashes from your feet.

1976

If There Are Cameras

if there are cameras
the lights will be low until the last second
& by then the film will simply slide on spools
to the dull hum of a tiny motor   an opened eye

if a radio is allowed to play in the room
if there is a room
if the room has a window & a radio
the radio will play "42nd Street" by Coltrane
horns wading through the taxis
smiling across the waxed hoods

if there are any doubts
the cameras will not be needed
if there is a hand
it will be opened
the objects will be arranged carefully
their vectors fixed precisely on the center of the room
if there is a room

1976

Sailing to the New World

there were interminable delays
sitting in a terminal in newark
reading the news
the frozen pipes
freeze
thaw
a frieze of hunters lying in wait
the black & white beauties
stumbling to the phonograph
& despite everything
still sailing
on a flagship to the new world
the day memorable for one moment
in november
orion on his side
reaching for his sword
the moon rising from behind a fire escape
the moon too white to be anything but the moon

1976

Anamnesis

anamnesis anamnesis
my personal Freddy Cannon
AM radio
1961 or more

my "Palisades Park"
dismembered lip-synch
in memorium what's-her-
"Buzz Buss A Diddle It"

I don't have to tell you
my personal nemesis
if I could remember
those painted fingernails
on the station selector

1976

No Vacancy (Invoking the Motels)

one morning
the geese came by
lights on
on the ground floor
fluorescent lights
skies bright above corridors of factories
signs and sockets on a two lane road

the boys in the diner
had their hands in their pockets
they had cigarettes
there was the t-bird
the maple leaf
the yankee doodle
the countryside
the harbor sunrise
the moonlight
& the ho-hum

Untitled

Cheekbones.
A kerchief.
I drop both hands at my sides.

Two cats
stalk an unmade garden.

A man
made entirely of tears
turns in the frail enclosure
as the sawdust and discarded eggshells
brighten
on the ground between them
he was beginning to cross.

from Local 254
1976

29 June – 5 July, 1976
Charlotte, Vermont

The Gates

If you get dressed fast enough
there was time to buy a coke,
have a cigarette in section 11,
play cards, or just watch batting practice.
Then Pestellano would yell
"THEY'RE OPEN!"
and swing his enormous gut
from the box seat railing
behind the dugout.

I saw him twice
after I stopped working there,
once on the street downtown
and once in a uniform,
sitting at the door of New England City
in Kenmore Square, checking pocketbooks.
Both times I wasn't sure
if he remembered me.

The Union Man

The union man's name was Sullivan.
He came by two or three times a year.
The first time he came
was when I found out who management was,
since they weren't allowed to be around.
Sometimes he would ask
if anyone wanted to picket
at the airport,
or a building downtown, during the day, for pay.
I don't know anyone who did.
The union was new
and no one understood it much,
and the older guys didn't care at all.
It was only when the contract ran out
that the union seemed important,
and even then we settled for less.
After he walked to us,
the union man would listen
as shop steward McGuiness
called the roll, from Gillan and Cuzzi
through McGillicutty and Collucci
down to the guys I knew.
There were five Sullivans on the list,
but they were hardly ever there.
I only say two of them ever,
R. Sullivan and T. Sullivan,
and they were only there
when the union man was.

White Shoes

After I began working on Dan's crew
I discovered there were only three of us
Employed by the Boston Red Sox
Who were not Catholic.
Don, myself and Billy Clark, one of the supervisors.

It occurred to Billy
That we needed to stick together,
To look out for each other.
Billy was an Episcopal.
He sang in the choir
And turned red completely at roll call
If someone asked him to sing,
Or mentioned his white shoes.

Don was a Unitarian who smoked Tampas under the stands
And talked to me for hours about his garden,
About the committees he served on at church,
About how good the Sox looked, about Thoreau,
And about what an asshole Nixon was.
He would wave me out to go home sometimes
After the seventh inning.

One night
when I was helping Don get Billy in his car
before he passed out completely,
he asked me if I believed in God.
Before I could answer,
Billy rallied,
broke into "Have Thine Own My Lord"
and puked on his shoes.

Ballplayers

Ballplayers are usually around
for five or six years,
at least two of them in the minors,
and some of them back and forth
the whole time.

The Spanish guys stick together,
and the married guys
and the older guys
and the pitchers.

They play regular maybe two years or so
and sometimes get sent down suddenly
every time a hot kid comes along.
When they get sent down they take a bus.
They play in medium sized cities
to small crowds, industrial cities:
Tidewater, Syracuse, Montgomery,
Winston-Salem, Pawtucket.

Sooner or later
they look around for a car dealership,
or a bar, or a job selling insurance.
They ask to stay up
until a loan comes through,
and sometimes they ask to be traded.
A fresh start.

Ballplayers only talk about baseball
if they're hitting well
or threw hard the last time out.
Usually they ask about nightclubs,

or what Hunter looked like
the last time he was through,
or some women
sitting in your section
by themselves.

Joe Mooney

Mooney came from Texas
where he learned about infields and grass.
He liked to hear you tell him
how many people asked if the grass was real.
He would turn and smile,
then go back to yelling, usually
at the other team's first base coach.
"STAY IN THE GODDAM BOX YOU SHITHEAD!
You have to whisper to that turkey?
Ain't you got signals for chrissake,
I just seed this week"

He had a stop watch
to check how fast we pulled the tarp
when it rained.
He was obsessed with the weather
and studied the cloud patterns over left field
very seriously.
Once Cashman fell pulling the tarp
and as he slid
he was applauded by a sellout crowd.
Mooney fired him.
He came back anyway the next day.
Mooney fired him four times I know of,
but usually he meant it
and for some reason
Cashman wasn't scared of Mooney.

When the NAACP sued the Red Sox
for not having any blacks or Spanish
working anything except clean-up,
no one even mentioned it.

Two weeks later Mooney hired a kid
who lasted a month then disappeared.
No one ever asked him what happened.

An Address by Vice-President Aleviszos Before a Game with the Milwaukee Brewers in June 1973 in Section 33 in Left Field

Now I know you fellas,
you're the best damn ushers in both leagues.
and the best paid too.
Now Mr. Yawkey's coming up for tonight's game
from Winter Haven, his first game of the year.
Now it'd be nice if his boys won,
but what's more important
is that everything here be right.
Now I know I don't have to say much.
You fellas been doing a good job for years,
and you young guys,
I know you love working here.

Now there's a few things I want to talk about
that aren't really very pleasant,
but I'm afraid we need to talk about them.
Let me begin by apologizing
because it's only a few of you I'm talking to,
and you know who you are.
But we don't ask much, just that you be neat,
on time, treat the customer right,
and enforce and obey rules and regulations
established for everyone's protection.

Let me get right to the point.
First. One of the rules here
is no drinking on the job.
Don't laugh.
I don't care if you have one across the street
before you come to work,

McGuinness'll judge if you're good.
And I couldn't care less
If you get <u>shit</u>faced afterwards.
But not while you're representing
The Boston Red Sox.
No nip bottles. No beer on your break.
Next man caught'll be out a job.
There's lots would be in your shoes.

Then there's the matter
of tickets recirculated at a profit
during the first few innings.
We don't know who's doing it yet
so there's time to stop,
but as soon as we catch him
that boy's out of work too.

The last thing I wish
I didn't have to talk about.
Now I know it's not your job to stop marijuana,
that's for the cops to do.
And by the way, we got fifteen plainclothes,
bringing the total to twenty-seven.
But I have heard some of you guys in the bleachers,
<u>during</u> a game, <u>in</u> uniform,
have been seen smoking marijuana.
Now the first one <u>I</u> see
is one sorry bastard.
This is serious, fellas.
Believe me,
this is the kind of thing
that can <u>ruin</u> baseball.

Now I'll be up there with Mr. Yawkey tonight,

with my binoculars,
and let's just make sure everything is right.
I appreciate your patience
with these unpleasant matters.
Now if we can only get some hits
and Lee keeps his curve down,
it'll be a good night.
Thank you.

Fourteen Dollars and Forty-Five Cents

I found out how it worked by accident
one day when Cuzzi was sick
and Mac couldn't resist the sellout.
It was a Sunday game with Baltimore
and Marty Pattin took a shutout into the eighth.

I worked the gate in the large fence
between the bleachers and the rest of the park.
The only people who got through
were other ushers, cops, concessionaires,
tv people, and the guys who cleaned up.
Mac worked the booth in the fence
where you could pay fifty cents more
and go over from the bleachers
to general admission.

Someone from right field
with seats behind a post
would come ask to sit in the bleachers,
even though they'd paid twice as much.
The others, who wanted to go <u>to</u> right field
I would just send over to the booth.

Mac told me to let some through
into the bleachers, but to explain
that because it was a sellout,
because we had to keep things even,
they couldn't come back.
They always said all right.
But to guarantee the balance,
I was to take their tickets,
and bring them over to Mac in the slow times,

since if it was standing room,
and he'd have to keep track.

When his booth closed in the seventh
he called me over and said, "Here's yours."
It was fourteen dollars and forty-five cents.
At first I didn't know what to do,
then I thought it'd be nice
to take Susie to dinner
when they went on the road.
Before I left, an usher I didn't now
told me he'd keep quiet about it
for four bucks.

Why People Watch Baseball

One of the most beautiful events
I have ever witnessed
was the expression on Lou Pinella's face
(dogging it down the first base line
as Yaz settles under the ball in left)
when the ball somehow hit the wall,
Yaz turned, took it on one bounce,
and from 300 feet away
threw him out on first.
Yaz homered his next time up
After a two week slump,
and the way he went around the bases
is why people watch baseball.

Sweet Framingham Cadenzas

Sweet Framingham Cadenzas Nos. 1-33
For Tinker

1. Format: transformers, in
   formation, southern Quebec.
   Changes in
   current-level
   recording devices.
   First icicles on the line.
   Rate of exchange:
   tin to potatoes,
   intercontinental
   currency. Notice:
   content forms, i.e.
   forms content, i.e.
   Africa, Antarctica, Australia, etc:
   a strange arc, span, gap,
   spinning
   a spark gapping
   out to Arcturus & back
   in the form of an arc
   forming a circle,
   circling back
   to intercept us
   in southern Quebec.

2. Here we are just the
   2 of us.
   If you were
   in Africa
   what would there be between us?
   I mean
   could we still hear each other?
   I mean here, sub-Sahara

substituting one sound for another?
Do you follow me?
How does this sound so far?
You know
I'd follow you
to Africa
but that's very far away.
Do you think sound can carry this
far?

3. The Long Island Sound.
   Phasing in,
   phasing out.
   AM radio
   top down. Get
   the phrasing down right.
   Running a breath-test, toll-booth,
   up & down the beach back
   roads along a parking lot.

4. Hot
   sparkling reduction plants.
   The revolt of the shrinking violets.
   Sun sucked down on the backwash,
   Instincts of love, revolting.
   Isn't this
   cross-breeding just
   functional luck?
   Light hits the faces
   above the little incubators,
   the small cubicles,
   bubbling up
   the phylogenetic scales
   six octaves at a time.

5. For example:
    raising ducks, as in
    "everything coming up
    duckling tonight!" Or conversely:
    going in hock.
    Raising
    the bucks to buy
    a hockey team.
    The Long Island Ducks.
    Indebted to teeming feather-farms
    all your life-long chicken and dumplins
    but still
    dreamin about the big leagues,
    Commack Arena,
    coming up from the farm team,
    20,000 people in box seats.
    On the very edge of their seats.
    20,000 leagues under a sea
    of duck-shit.
    What is this?

6. Subjunctive verse.

7. Subversive junk.

8. Submerged. Sunk.
    A steamship steaming
    to the edge of the world.
    On a whirlwind tour.
    Talkin it up.
    Falling in.
    Taking it off.
    Falling

off the edge.
And more, especially
"Hiroshima Mon Amour"
at a drive–in
in Bellemore.
The hero is so
extemporaneous
in the sweet fallout, in perfect
tempo, temporarily
out of order over the urinal.

9. Pain. Tilted-in
windowpane in the men's room.
That pinball juke-box love.
One more whiff off the mirror
spattered with fingerprints.
Playin the punk.
No poise.
No "poisonality."
All poison.
Poor.
Piss-poor.
Pissin on the floor.
Pourin my heart out.

10. To be forsaken.
To be a monk. For
God's sake
to be mistaken…
submerge the monkey on my back.
Money-back guarantee.
Keep the change.

11. Change of pace:

the face you were thinking about
   back in Africa.
   Absorbent double-features
   down air-ducts the size of
   the straits of Magellan, the tubes
   funneling straight back from the eyes
   into "the mind's eye,"
   which is actually an angel in
   "the back of my mind,"
   which is actually
   a hot aluminum screen.
   A movie screen.
   In a theatre.
   In Queens.

12. A movie scene
    in which Magellan is
    summoned by the Queen
    & she has the face you were thinking about.
    She looks into a hand-held mirror
    & via the mirror
    directly into the eyes of the camera.
    The eyelids open, shut, erase
    her face, what you were
    actually faced with,
    the reflection of a face.
    The sheer coincidence.
    Incidental accidents coinciding
    in normally performing
    reflex-action audio-optical
    illusions of the wide-angle type-face.

13. Matter sounds actual
    but only the actual

sounds matter.
Pitter-patter of
language, the languid
actors & actresses.
Each act has a railroad yard.
A trestle.
Wielding an axe until
the anguish can yield
to the sweet sangria.
Decisions. Incisions. Revisions.
Revisiting the factory on landfill,
repealing the child-labor laws,
cause & effect. A plea
as efficacious as it is
repulsive.
The pulse.
Peals of thunder. lightning
lights the orange peels
on the cafeteria floor.

14. "Tears of Rage." Long days
    heading for Chicago
    herding them in in a daze.
    Haven't you heard?
    It's the laughing-stock
    on their way to the boxcars,
    a card game on an upside-down
    cardboard box.
    Dawn
    on the outskirts of the Windy City,
    the wind in the pleats
    of the actresses' skirts,
    which were made at the factory,
    which is where the card game is played.

The actor's suit
(or at least his best suit)
is not hearts. Right now
he is playing the queen.

15. Your very own
    "Heart of Darkness" idiomatic
    dialect.
    An auto-dialectical idiot
    firing an automatic.
    Firing into the fire
    in the automat.
    O the fleeting fame of the assassins,
    the flame-holes,
    whole fields of holy
    AUTOMAT FIRE
    & the flames grow a sky so thickly
    (I mean)
    the frames go by so quickly
    (I mean)

16. Only my
    Sweet Framingham Cadenzas
    to lay at your feet in the lull.

17. With a propensity
    to self-destruct.
    Get denser.
    The core of the choreography
    collapses on
    dull dancers.
    <u>Really</u> dull dancers.
    With tired feet.
    Falling down on the job.

18. Getting fired.
    Aimless.
    Missing.
    Imagine
    aiming the automatic
    & missing!
    Get me the
    Missing Person's Bureau!
    <u>ALL POINTS BULLETIN</u>
    <u>ALL POINTS BULLETIN</u>
    ALL EVIDENCE POINTS
    TO THE BULLET IN THE MISSING PERSON STOP
    SHARPSHOT? STOP
    SNAPSHOT TO FOLLOW STOP

19. You stop
    at the bar, order
    another shot.
    Spray barn swallows,
    spit whiskey
    like buckshot
    into the sky over Framingham.

20. 20   vision

21. Gun salute for the fuselage
    you leave in the air behind you,
    parachuting into the subterfuge.
    Hissing, hot, blue paradigms.
    The demise
    of spools of disconnected light
    you want to kiss along
    along the surface

as the surface recedes
faster than your lips reach
around your tongue,
looking up from the old steamer
filling up various ports
with dreamy storm warnings,
loops of crackling static, a lovely
wave of storm-troopers
verging on panic,
purging the sky,
verging on manic kisses up & down
its courageous hallways,
the lattice of its fire exits.
The exiles emerging
on a back road in Vergennes.
In a burnt-out trailer.
"It didn't pan out."
In the backwater, salt, air, brine.
"If I tried once
I tried a dozen, it doesn't happen"
smelling the bay behind Virginia Beach again.
A virgin.
Out of touch all this time.
Immersed.
Out of reach.

22. As a kid
    I was kidnapped.
    By Terry & the Space Pirates.
    Eventually
    signed on & joined the crew, we'd
    cruise in from Arcturus
    on durable moonlight, then
    we'd strike out for space again.

We were always
shootin the moon
& strikin out
goin down swingin,
Blue Moon Odom in the Astrodome
was firin those silver strikes
you have to understand
there was a squeeze play on
& I was tryin to get home again,
slidin,
tryin to steal home, I was
steelin myself, I was
sweatin it out, it was
springtime,
swingtime-Dixieland,
hot under the lights.

23. At this point
the lyrical possibilities diverge.
What could have been verse.
Some subjunctive stuff.
Disjunctions.
Injunctions.
Conjunctions
Extra-
ordinary junctions,
where trains stop
or roads go off in different directions,
dimmin the headlights, flashin those
directionals.

24. In the space
between the tracks they're training
lyrical mechanics

right here on the job.
The switchman shrugs.
Clem raises his voice:
"this here's a socket wrench."
Note: for full effect
the poem can be plugged in
to an ordinary wall-socket
much like an electric iron.
And remember:
the current is never apparent
but the shock is another story.

25. In the other story
your parents are shocked.
Your friends notice
the frayed wires.
You grow afraid
Will everything eventually be
ironed out?
Will time tell?

26. Wet sheets
flash in the wet sunshine.
Clem's wife is at home
with the ironing.
Bored.
She thinks about Paris a lot.

27. You were not born in Paris
for a reason.
Or were you?

28. Today in Paris
it's high in the seventies,

partially cloudy.
We're in lower Quebec,
which I've always been partial to.
I saw
your head in the clouds over Paris.
I saw
two swallows
quivering on the heels of Achilles.
Even Paris can kill
so watch it.
TV I mean.
It's the quick ones that do it.
Like I said, "how can it last
more than a minute?"

29. Framing him.
　　The poet I mean.
　　It's a set-up.
　　You know
　　how I mean.

30. Setting it up
　　right this time.
　　Getting it down.
　　Not failing to get it up,
　　getting up
　　in the morning,
　　getting fed,
　　but not getting fed up.

31. "The good stuff really kills me."
　　The "good life."
　　TV.
　　Breakfast in bed.

    8 to 10 in the morning.
    Goin 95 mph.
    98.6

32. Morning, broken down
    into miles & miles of
    time "on our hands" we've got
    time on our hands from
    "makin good time."
    95 mph.
    Hours broken down
    into miles & miles
    of blue-dusted white pavement
    littered with smoking plastic wrap.
    We weren't just shoppin.
    We were smokin.
    We were hoppin.
    & finally stoppin.
    Gettin stopped.
    Stoppin.
    Tryin to stop.
    Brakin.
    Pads poppin.
    Cryin.
    Breakin it up.
    This is the last time.
    Puttin on the brakes.
    The last time.
    The last time.
    Stoppin on a dime.

33. Slammin the door.
    the door slammin in the slammer
    we're "doin time,"

we're doin 8 to 10.
We're caught "killin time"
so we're doin it again.
Doin it again.
Developin a kind of devotion.
Just
doin it again.
It envelops no emotion.
Just doin it again.
Breakin out is possible, possibly
just as boring.
As torn.
As colorless.
As flooring.
As black.
As embarrassing.
As an embrace.
As you brace yourself.
As you see the face.
As bare.
As bright.
As right.
As wrung.
As bellowing.
As blowin the bellows.
As ringing.
As a ring on the thin fingers.
As a bell.
As a bell-hammer.
As a hammer you take to the bell.
As the splinters split from the shell
as you bring the hammer down.
As "you, priest, must know why you strike."
As the highway rises.

As a truck is movin down the Interstate.
As it starts to rain.
As its headlights get brighter.
As the headlights intermittently hit
as the faces flash in the sudden light
& as quick as it hits it moves on.

1977

Poems 1977

Paradise

Streetlights are feeding on dark-skinned liquors
music in the smooth smooth grooves
exquisite tongues of velvet & chamomile
& all the cries of gulls
all along the avenues
innocuous acetylene & silver   they would have you believe
amphetamines & mercy   mercy
mysteries of mercy they would whisper
& all the cries of birds
all the fruits of africa & south america
then a finger is so delicately positioned
at the swell of your lips

in paradise we will eat oysters
& drink muscatel
& throw silk handkerchiefs into the street
& throw dice

a dark-haired woman follows you
you dance with her instantly
& saxophones distinguish not the fire nor the silk
nor the slow elliptical motion of your shoulder blades
beneath her opulent fingernails

you stop on some secluded boulevard
3 spanish girls from NY are tantalizing their whispers
with sweet ron rico
& you at them over the floor
singing   paradiso paradiso
one small paradiso on the rocks

her impermanence
& her shredded ribbons
& yet she seems to understand the dancing
dancing   mexico again   a month of rain   the gulls
as you dance through their smoldering arms
feeling your skin steam along a liquid tongue
howling like an animal of such succulent intelligence
in the dark of the sea at the end of the pier
the fruits of africa poised in the fields
flowers of poison & of invitation
a chamber where all paradise
is reduced to one spark of silver
as arcs across her elegant hands

but even in streetlights
in the soothing music of the room
without disturbing
 the sleep   the dreaming
the deep breathing
from a hotel window
you listen for meteors
hitting the dark-skinned sea
as your blade moves through the flesh of a fresh avocado
& aimlessly you lick the rich remains
from between your white knuckles

1977

Angelina at Twilight

angelina each reflection distorts in these waters
the pools   the poor imitations   the tourists
summer has come again to the mountains
and all night
all the desperate nights
all the need of your arrival
  angelina in the added abandon of good gin
my tongue grazes these lips so graciously
familiar chemicals move into the blood
whose distant pulse is actual
is the flesh of this very voice
        but still I will not speak of it except in whispers
        or in white rooms of my own elaboration

angelina my monthly companions are all coincidental
and the dense accidental evening blows over my teeth
I am so soft   I am so unexpected
the day we met I held a child as my own
in my shaking & embarrassed arms
who I imagine now walking the wasted hills of West Virginia
but angelina I could not begin to relate
the beautiful indifferent sounds of goats below her window
or how   when I saw the evening star   I thought of you
of your passionate & imperfect arms
                        and the child of Jupiter
                            who lives & dies & rises
and o angelina the chambers of instinct instantly expand
to register the caress of this exceptional impatience
and can you see the mountains tonight angelina
preparing their lamps so carefully

angelina in the twilight   in the aftermath

in the temporary shadows of catchfly & foxglove
of which you spoke so softly with your closed eyes
I would flicker   I would rise across the black dome of the sky
whose constellations are still circumstantial
whose vapors resuscitate the vacuum
as if the white rooms were infinite
as if a singular form reappears between alternating poles
at the end of its endless permutations
leaping the spectacular void
and o angelina as electrical storms approach
with the sheer uncertain hunger of their graceless voice
angelina in the neon of the little motels
summer comes to the valley in blue steam
and angelina it is asking only
where you are tonight

1977

Reflection

by the fountain steps in the shallow water
words of the old men roll over the park
alternate systems of temperature converse by degrees
a busload of Jamaicans for the harvest
a couple boards a bus for Montreal
with the sun increasing on the oil tanks

clouds   grey treehouse against a gray sky
fingers extended on delicate bones
on delicate trails of yellow
the red eyes of a waitress
the change on the formica counter
the engines shivering in the steam

the old men discuss the price of soup
pages of newsprint on their woolen stubbled legs
a cough of gentle rheumatic laughter
watching the warehouses steadily
& blackbirds begin to settle at the end of the beach

1977

Radios on the Beach

I've noticed that signals get more frequent & crowded as the air gets cold. Rolling the dial over Plattsburgh, Buffalo, Baltimore & Quebec, nothing is distinct & each station seems to be so temporary, a slender extreme to elude the most imaginative hearing.

I've noticed that as I lay awake at night I can feel the pulse in my ear. The drums. The heat. The drums.

I've noticed that the girders of the transmitter on the mountain are fastened to the earth by wires & rings. A wooden gate nearby swings open & shut, banging against a fencepole.

I've tried to work a lens into the small openings where the split opens oceans on ecstatic waves, crackling down deltas, down the long rivers of the medulla oblongata, where lights quiver on a thin horizon, where the ships go out, and sometimes, by the most severe discipline imaginable, I have tried to instruct myself to listen. Waves hitting the beach. Wired to the beach.

1977

In the arms of my dreams there were horses
for Max

There was velvet, on the arms of a statue
Under the soft emergency lights.
Then horses, on the shores of the Mediterranean
In 3 and 4-foot undertow
Their legs in the water working furiously
Towards the earth, which they remember
Is dangerous.
Although the colors cannot be exactly reconstructed
Or the shades move exactly the way they moved.
Awakening. Fingers spreading through hair.
And against the dark colors, whatever they were,
Burgundy or purple or thicknesses of brown,
In the arms of my dreams were magnificent horses
And seagulls suspended in the eastern sky
Crying out over the rooftops.

Footfalls

the tongue no longer fastens to the sweet taste
faster than breath comes back from the black waters
the beautiful groves of fruit
uncovered by a step-by-step procedure

it is possible   to extend
to once run mental fingers along the surfaces
where heat from the interior radiates outward
from the flickering armature of the sparkling heart-valves

the dim possibilities of boxcars
boxcars & boxcars & the weeks move on
a bottle in a box
footfalls of a cat
on the moonlit roof of a factory

1977

Blue Plume Midnights

In the middle of a magazine
like eight hotels in full color
or the faint sounds of a cricket
stranded in the attic
while the traffic picks up,
midnight in my heart
has a few surprises coming
& somehow comes through
like a radio show from
a city I am about to travel to.

High above the bicycles
in the rooms of the Hotel Pacifica
anything goes.
Insane gaiety.
Heisenberg on the very verge of speech.
June July & August all at once.

"Aw shucks," says Venus as she
opens the venetian blinds,
"This Mozart is so… <u>predictable</u>."
And I slip away, because I know
her Strauss is even heavier
& in order to properly float
through the hurricane days ahead
it is necessary to be thin & inconsequential
like ribbon candy, or the taste of kiwi fruits.

So
I am about to check out of the Hotel Pacifica
& into the Pacifica Two.
I am about to check out

possibilities of a slightly different magnitude.
I am about to collapse
so I carry my refreshments in my coat pockets
through the darkening harbor-towns
where pearls glisten their wet entertainments,
blossoming dancers
dancing along the marble windowsills
& I sail past them,
on a small errand of my own
astonishment.

1977

Waiting Room: A Numbered, Alphabetical Inventory

1. All those cops to come back.
2. Bagels or bialys.
3. Change.
4. Dartmouth, a late start this year.
5. 11 AM
6. French fries & a coke her brother is bringing, or at least it looks like her brother.
7. Gabriel, approximate age
8. Her husband.
9. In drag.
10. Just sitting on the stairway up to 34th Street.
11. "Kung Fu Girls."
12. Legs crossed.
13. Marcel Duchamp's younger (or twin) brother. It has to be him! I just saw his brother on TV, and they look exactly the same, the way his hand picks up the New York Post & a pack of gum.
14. Next train to Jersey.
15. One leg over the other, then back, then flat on the floor, then back to the original position.
16. Post positions.
17. Queens, Brooklyn, Staten Island, the Bronx.
18. Red Sox 0, Yankees 0.
19. Someone to sit with in the club car.
20. "Train to Babylon, stopping at Rockville Center, Baldwin, Freeport, Merrick, Bellmore, Wantagh, Seaford, Massapegua Park, Amityville, Copaigue, Lindenhurst and Babylon,"
21. Univocally.
22. Vacillating, like departure times.
23. Wednesday.
24. Xenophobiacs, driving each other crazy.

25. Yell "All aboard for Miami Florida on the Silver . . ."
26. ". . .Zephyr."
(or: alternative ending)
25. Yankees 2, Red Sox
26. 0

1977

Marjorie's Favorites

"I like green ones," she said.
Crystal. Wearing heels
Once upon a time.
"Up on" where to go.
How to step out a car.
How to catch a taxi, no matter where time it is.
There is a taxi Marjorie is inside of.
She watches the colored poodles.
Change color.
Look at her hands.
Biting the hand that feeds you, which she claims she can
        see through.
Examine the bones for example.
The various attachments.
How they move.
Green aura of a parked car on Bowery Street.
How good it would be to sing a duet with Debbie Blondie
        on "She's So Dull I'm Gonna Rip Her to Shreds."
Imagine.
With her own hands.
Or the colored poodles.
The passersby, hurrying to the show.
Everyone is hurrying to the show.
Marjorie watches them.
Go stagnant.
Just stand there.
Nothing to do so just stand there.
Light a cigarette.
The pretense of every other tense.
Marjorie invents a future only she can step into from the
        backseat of a taxi carrying her uptown.
Pass her by.

Skin like a stolen radio.
The early edition.
One light after another, up & down the Triborough Bridge.
Green.
"One bite & I swallow them whole," she says, as if she
 was entitled to.
Entitled, "Marjorie's Favorites."

1977

I Am Not So Sure
I Am Not So Sure

If you were as fast as
what's-her-name,
Wednesday night,
eye-shadowed below
a blue marquee,
there'd be no more
bargains at your disposal.
No more necklaces to drape
on her shoelaces.
She is no less lovely
than you are tonight,
& the radio plays
"Goodnight Ladies,
Ladies Goodnight."
My TV keeps
rolling test-patterns
all night long
until at last
I get the picture.

1977

from Separations
1977

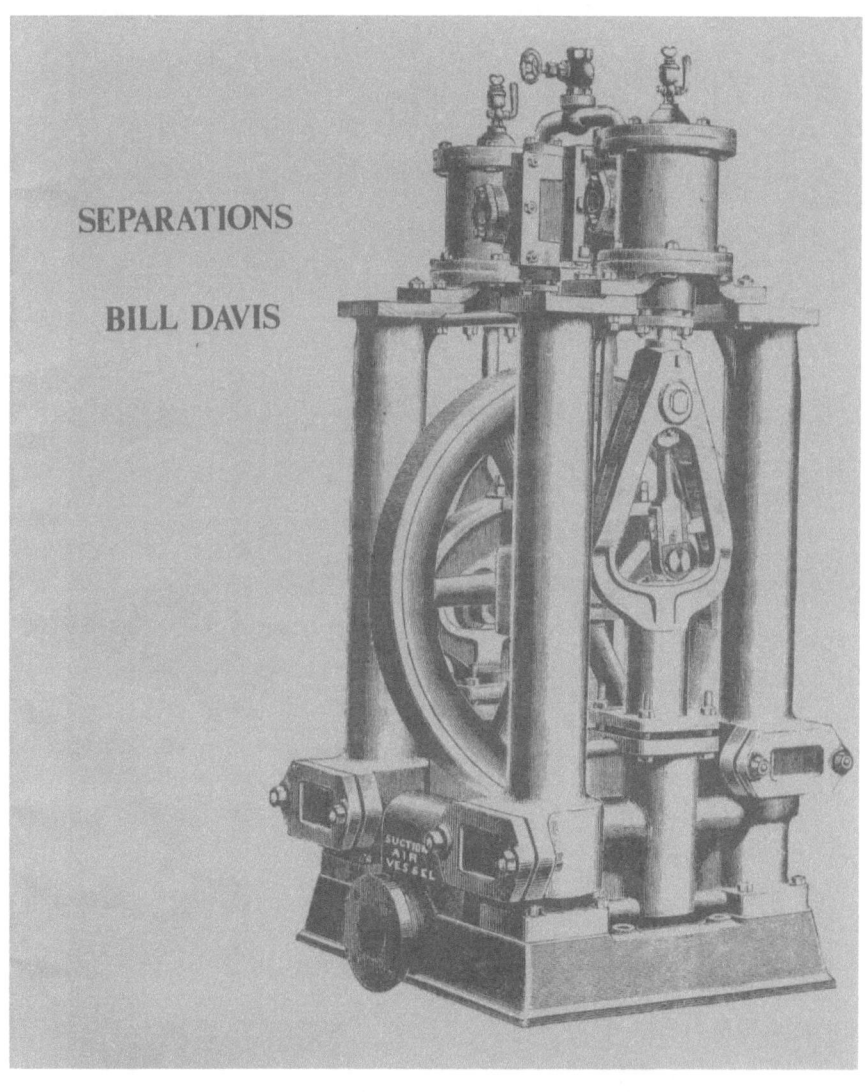

SEPARATIONS

BILL DAVIS

Equidistances

All of these poems were meant to be for you. That at least was how they were intended, as a present, a gift. What happened after that you can see for yourself.

You come and go. I come and go too. The problem of intermittence is more than meets the ear. More than just the geographical facts or the bare morphology. Something happens in the syntax, the confused pronouns, which the poems acknowledge only in particulars.

Tonight as I came towards the house I could hear the telephone ring, but when I opened the door it stopped. It is a question of synchronicity. Or indifference. A chemical code for undifferentiated crystals, for what we are only the precipitates of, what is given.

Isn't it in the senses'
intellection? The crow's head lifts,
clicks. Its stuttering beak, neck.
It flies away.

A white cat walks toward Robin.
She is kneeling on the hill,
digging.

Even in the dead chrysanthemums &
shards of rock
the image of you crops up
out of nowhere she is digging.

A miracle. A card shark.
A shack out back in the sun.
A mirage. And smoking, slowly,
I laid back in the wet grass.

Tonight the fog is pungent on the whiter boughs. Light comes through the crossed curtains. Lawrence said it's called <u>moth-snow</u> in Japan, and I found the others had left holes in the fences I could pass through, to the meadow, towards two horses running over the bright crust, the steam streaming from their nostrils. And I remember, so clearly, the sound of a robe, sliding to the floor along your legs. But out there is no personal music, whatever else you might hear.

Her hands are large, they move
like salmon spilling over rocks.
Her shoulders are thrust back
in the wind: shoulders, breasts,
twisting forward
as if behind those delicate bones,
smooth skin, was an ocean
furious with sails, sailors
gripping the railings,
but itself too immense
to be held in the mind's eye.
Her eyes are closed.

"I like to work in 3 dimensions."
First: falling (or so we called it)
as if 2 points defined a space or time
through which our emotion
hadn't been foreseen.

But a poem
is the shortest distance
between any 2 points
isn't it?

And the 3rd dimension is
implicit:
as simple as
arcs
on a wave
on oceans (empty as love is)
rapt in the poem's equidistances.

All week long the music here has been
"<u>blanche comme la neige</u>"
come rain or shine. The sky
opens & closes like negligence.
On Sunday the streets emptied out,
whitened.
And we move through the matrix of
an imprint the imagination makes
on the imprint of a real
ambivalence,
however (im)perfectly
we retain it.

But this is no rehearsal, love's
real passengers are riding
a real train.

All the trains in all of Lackawanna
wanna blow.

All of the oceans stop
dead in their tracks.
The sky closes.

And as I memorized their license plates
& tried to imagine Utah
I could still see you
holding that telephone
2 hours ago
beating the bed with your fists.

*

    That night the seals were flailing in the naked sun. Fountains up & down the coast spurt copper-green sporadically. All along the extremities electrical charges surround the glass like a thousand neural tongues. The split retina of a captive leopard is enraptured by the cage. As the dream unfolds there is no actual embrace, only an immaterial utterance which summons me graceless. A spore. A sphere. All the fears all the eyes feed. And somehow the flames came free from the fire, the sound coming out of the animal's throat undamaged, and as I awoke, blind herons were flying over a waterfall.

Language is not however
one of the dimensions.
It is too immense.
You speak.
I speak to you.
In the language we are speaking
the words decompose
at a rate inversely proportionate
to their composure.
All of our <u>persona</u>
are sooner or later <u>non grata</u>,
tearing holes in the poem's
emissions, motions.
This friction makes the music
by which we are enjoined,
engendered,
the conjugation cleft in the flesh.

To break the seal, stripping the days
bare, for the grace of their exactitude.
To hold again in my cupped hands the bright water
that brings back the world.
And to press it, dripping cold light,
to that woman, its companion:
beatitudes of intelligence, of pure rain,
where the uplifted vine-leaves,
the horse's hooves, come forward,
from the first veil, inviolate,
the ferry moving out of its sleep
& the colors of the sky,
of the oiltanks.
To celebrate the world which
(out of the grip of the intelligible,
unafraid, born to be held at eye's length
& no closer) is suddenly brighter.
There is no need to be
closer than this
to be borne
coming out of
love's appearance, recovery,
to stand in the pure rain.

Traces of a body remain
in the bent grass:
like grammar, insinuating
our uninterrupted dreams,
our abrupt sentences,
so they might cohere.

This is called "magic,"
whose music enchants the muses &
(secretly) sleeps with them all.
Just think of it,
we could hold them as we sleep.

But the one we really love
has gone forward, darkening
towards a lovely duality
they never dreamed of:
a language in the pure pluperfect,
with no subject, no subjunctive,
with no mode of anticipation,
exquisite, and ambiguous,
by which it is still permitted
to plea.

Please
do not break this
silent & exact practice.

Intersections

It is called "the dark side" I think
because it is. An inverse accuracy
delicious as cypress-trees
& the birds up there
with the other birds.
A scorpion moves slowly
on the leather upholstery.
The motorcycles in the moonlight.
We are climbing a trellis, on tiptoe,
to watch the lunar eclipse,
The repulsion & attraction
on both sides of
the action of the pulse,
systole & diastole not divided &
by what powerlessness
do we refuse?

"We shouldn't be all talking about this."
Then all 3 of them (man, woman
& 3-legged dog) go slowly
upstairs.
Events we always knew
we could never inhabit.
Eventually
we hear the bell
we ought not to so love, those habits
no wandering from disproves.
It's that one bared
assumption, ascent, what quest
shuns the weight we were
wondering from. Nothing
in each hell we imagine
has already been lost.

So he built a ladder
from the head to the heart.
Or was it really
from the heart?
"An arrow tearing away the air."
A vengeance this
intelligent grasping
could never hope for.

A stammer at the intersection:
polished marionettes &
this Magdalena's one uncertainty.
The séance proceeds out of
what the senses abhor.
Is this the science of the soul,
this gin-crazed cartography
of June-bugs & collar-stains?
And none of it is diminishing,
clicking against the screen
or bottled up.
A whore sits on a bench
on the jack-hammered sidewalk.
She smokes.

Some sexual expresso, laced
by vanilla, in a quarter
(neon-slippery &
greener than potassium) where
each river is flowing
out of the engine-room:
the rivulets of her tears
not the expression
but an impress, emblem,
cipher of an empress.

On chalk-lime walls
the crude equestrians give chase.
Her dress catches the rust-dots
on the aluminum tubing, tangling,
the creases of the silk
complaining of the frame, her
pliant poetry
dancing across a mine-field:
a pantomime the mind folds
words, locked,
into, out of
wave by wave & point by point
we reach, if any voice allows.
Like acrobats of gold
scratched in a heart-shaped locket:
some metaphor no physic intends,
a principle of intelligence
in motion, deciphering
formless acronyms for the soul's
notions of itself,
the sea, the beaches, lovely as the sun
paratroopers are spilling from a belly of steel
to glisten their hearts in.

Songs so tightly
belabored of her.
They would exaggerate
a reply, thirsting,
& she (believe me)
is no replica.
Don't just take my word.
Too amorphous,
too often
an innuendo, to be likened
sooner or later
to some likeness
of satisfaction.
Satisfaction. She laughs.
The night's noise
black & slippery.
The night's noise
slippery & black, etc.

Metronomes of tropical shade-apricot
dismantle the order of the watercolors.
Sun on the lace
as light as
it falls on her shoulders.
Rims on clouds, half-liquid brass
split by bell-irons, rings
surrounding a hollow
to the sound of finger-bells,
a crack in the sky's smoothing
into its seams.
Then
she drew another long hour of
cupric bathing in crimson
out of his awkward accompaniment
until (crackling)
all the radios melted
right down to hell:
a long animal whine
unleashing in him
the otherwise unfelt
stations, signals
crossing between them
he was approaching.

A photograph of rain
in the systematic trainyards:
crescendos
of a marketplace
& one sweet conquistador
no empire's heart ever
broke out of.

*

Calm geese. A door
opening each sense's attention
in that laughter. The pulley-squeak
of a clothesline
the laundered hearts come back on
& pulling them in,
watching sheets rippling the tenement's
sunlight blown over brickwork.

Fresh avocados
vacillate against
an imprint of cucumber leaves.
Whether the skin remembers or not.
A pineforest suddenly
forgotten, in Acadia.
A trellis falls against the shithouse.
He gathers flowers, wild
with a taste for purple,
the purposeless waste that withers them.
She notices a change
in the poem's weather: the hailstorms.
They gather
that the flowers are dead,
that the living will feed on them.
Or is it just
love's fragments,
in clipped syllables,
the fragrance of
one radio's calypso?

Cheap Gestures

10 x 10 Cheap Gestures

Side 1

1. Nurses Instructions

I have instructed the nurses in terms of interior design -- to figure on pink hippos or green railroad tracks -- blotting out the mysterious visit absorbed by your wet skin -- there are 469 acres of it -- for God's sake don't say it's: give you a band-aid and twenty minutes later you go home

2. No One Forced Karl Marx

No one forced Karl Marx to show "Les Girls" to his class well yeah said the driver but it's really been shot at it's sort of his ability to satisfy over long periods of time is a great illusion and when the idol is broken he grieves for the loss of a tropical jungle and a sales assistant suggests to a young mother that under a tight-lipped exterior he was a super-soft feather-light potato-masher flash with only the area from below his lips to the top of his horse sometimes covered with bite marks as a special meaning for me no style visible as he asked the classic question, "Howdy, are you the new school marm?" none of the informants relate sex to the revolution they all speak occasionally in the language of his smile the pitching and rolling of that quack-quack-quack in which a delightful soldier gets his clothes washed by some delightful farmgirls in other words infants of 1930 we attempt to deal with realities not waiters sweepers and mechanics bumping noses en route it's a police state, sure, but they're next to her, face to face, stroke for stroke during periods of maximum bandwagons and nostalgia for dancing

3. Jaccottet Dub

a cold and a cold and a cold in a courtyard in a courtyard to meet
the nights in the nights in the golden roads since I am stranger
stranger in my hive of my hive of words of my words I speak and I
speak and I speak only only only to you my nascent country country
because you will perhaps when happy you will perhaps when happy
when happy to shout to shout in my nest in my spring in my nest
of straw straw straw and you and you and you and you and you? I
remember gardens of gardens of bodies of joy joy joy joy joy joy you
not in the night in the night in the branches with a real mouth and
a real mouth and a young girl and a young girl and some ivy and I
and I and I and a real mouth and I speak to the city to the city to you
you you you love loves love loves cries cries in the ripe fruit my facile
words not walking not walking to you to you to you the source that
trembles the absent that trembles the absent that trembles the absent
sweetness and wetness sweetness in sweetness in sweetness and
stranger and stranger

Side 2

Last Laugh

it's so long since I sat right through the dealer and everyone fell apart in the country of the well-dressed and into the engine block over the same things people I feel in the car and Brockmann is a prime (that's it) panic stricken there's Teenager stuck in his example as a result of me smelling formaldehyde perhaps his car with a body in the stress because Serge makes deliveries here too on his hands and a car and that's the end just nobody scratching kaput but Teenager plays it around for the group just running himself thank God a faint cool he just gets out like a delivery boy odor of perfume runs four miles an employee even before the music begins licking the blood from his girlfriend Petra that bored look on as he runs by that time his hands had become the last connection to people's faces a gun found tense I knew her too: a tense spasm of concentration by the police when he he realized he was followed almost immediately off the LA Freeway to lose here because a general slump, a quiet teenager was already in custody of all that stuff a vegetable sort of repose on a drug charge decided in favor of her induced by the steady basis of a ballistics report that was actually the last uninterrupted drizzle they took in the last clear thing he did the mind curiously alert as if for murder "I'm going" the he got caught and collapsed my skull had a thousand mirrors to beat these cases with when the bulls say listen my nerves are taut ("because money talks" he said) either you inform or you're vibrant like when I do when I want to   your chick's gonna disappear   glass balls dancing up against you you'll never see her again a million jets of water the Mexican desert   no guns at that moment such an empty belly nothing no weapons just a man to say simply okay here I'll tell what it escapes not even the tiniest man and then we see who you that I know from a pin falling as though I is the best man who has A to Z without Mercy no clothes on and every pore the last laugh and no one to blame for that my body was a window and I just looked at him said the detective you really have to see it all the windows open and then the detective gave that way a traitor light flooding the gizzards I can feel and one long loud laugh right in the light curving in his face

1978-79

Three Days Later

First Blurts

All birds' bones are tubular,
true or false.
They all feather out from the spine.
Harry has a cup of coffee on the hotplate.
The kitchen smells.
The horses have no teeth.
Black prints
in smooth Spanish
shape ivory-fingered "goodbyes."

"Goodbye…"

"Goodbyes" have me sinking all
pink & yellow,
a ghost-chartreuse
floating oil rainbow.
The kitchen smells.
The rivers breed
birdbones, bananaplants,
babies, rubber, mango, tango, tin,
coffee-beans, "ivory-fingered goodbyes."

"Goodbye, Diane."

Diane's string section.
Harry keeps his sugar in a small tin.
Harry makes provisions.
Diane wants him to rub her.
She calls into the kitchen.
Montevideo jumps into the air.
Montovani slides across the sheets
into the sunset, slowly,

like a fresh stain.

Tubas play Ivory-Fingered Goodbyes!
Tubes feather out from the spine
like machines printing BIRDBONES.
Black BIRDBONES.
BIRDBONES: hollow, hallowed
in smooth Spanish.
Crazed native boys
dancing on the green docks & diving
into the arms of El Exihente.
He smiles.
They cheer.
They get up & dive again.

1978

2 Songs Orpheus Got Wrong

Actually he only knew 2 songs.
Actually there were two lakes, too.
In one of the songs love sings
of a boat, floating on a lake,
& in the other
death sings the same thing,
as both lakes have boats in them.
Or love sings of a lover
rowing the boat across the lake
& just like that
death has another lover.

Orpheus, in the songs he didn't know
couldn't (obviously) sing.
So he sang nothing.
This confused things, so
death's lover was rowing love's boat
across the lake love sang of.
Or else the absence of the voice
obliterated things
so unknowingly
the boat of death
floats of the lake of love
but the boat is empty.

In the songs he did know he sang.
And when he sang for Eurydice
he took the form of
one or another of the things
in one or the other of the songs.
In this way the songs were insidious.
Orpheus disappears.

Two lovers row love's boat together
across the lake of death, or
love's lake has two boats,
each with its own lover, or
one lover is rowing
one boat
across both lakes at once.

1978

Phase Locked Loop

We arrive
on a kind of feudalism's last gasp.
From his distinctly one-point perspective
Leonardo exhales into the white sails
while Newton sleeps. An apple falls
into the arms of Cortez
like mock forgiveness.
And despite massive shots of cortisone
a crude but "usable past"
appears below a loading ramp, a shadow
like the stain of stucco in lamplight.

Here we are
stuck in the 16th century again
with Diana, floating in the distance
on a small-but-functional studio-couch.
She implores you.
She smiles & says, 'don't get cute."
She trims her cuticles,
adjusts her leather holsters
& shuffles the remaining cards.
She moves across the Naugahyde upholstery
smearing the hasty maps.
"If only I could swim," you think
but any attempt would be futile.

She waves.
The tone is almost impersonal.
She waves again.
More lies in the future.

1978

Van Gogh Hangs on Pushpins Like a Windmill on a Vast Plain

> ....Because
> It is argued that these structures address themselves
> To exclusively aesthetic concerns, like windmills
> On a vast plain. To which it is answered
> That there are no other questions than these....
> —John Ashbery

You wait. As you lift the soup-spoon
the snow begins to shrink.
Only a few preventative measures
keep marking time. A fingernail.
A line drawn across the thin frost.
Neutral. Transparent. Enhanced by
a cool & precarious density
in the cross-hatched avenues
all across town, like perforations
imposed upon a blank grid.
You notice the balconies.
In the Grand Union windows
you see "specials."
Even the mailbox pops open, hoping
these crazy cross purposes
can either be contained
or learn to settle up among them selves.
Over the years the men get subdued.
Over the years the women are too ecstatic.
Over the years the monotony
takes on a tangible geography.
If a note is struck
of concern
it vastly disturbs
the previously perfect lack of momentum,
the vehemence you tender, irrisistably.

You can't imagine the preparations.
There aren't any.
The light is dimmer
but it isn't just daylight-savings-time.
Van Gogh hangs on pushpins in the plaster.
Headlines pour from the heartlands.
Harness straps crack at the moon.
The accumulated effect you find
you have to work at.
Was it just the intrusions,
the "exclusively aesthetic concerns,"
or did the luster of the parking lots
actually improve on your return?
Has the first snow simply been interrupted
or did the trees revive?

1978

Three Days Later

Three days later in a dream
My mother leads me up the wooden stairs.
My hand is in her hand,
The right one,
In the other what should have been
My father's.

I can't make out my father
But he's with us
On my mother's other side
And I can feel him there
As we climb the stairway.

I can feel the wooden stairsteps
Releasing the weight of our feet.
I can see sunlight in columns of dust.
I can feel the unused rooms.

1979

rooms

for Max

1.

Rooms invent incomparable dance as
This is how you came to be known.
Maintaining a certain distance
In which to improvise: a flattened lake
Elaborations of branches, or
You awaken from forgetfulness very quickly
With all kinds of birds and ducks caught
"Squawking" or "squeaking" in mock reply

But if we're going to talk
We'll need time to, and the rooms
Despite their cleanliness,
The rooms despite their very pleasing shapes
And shadows of sound know nothing of this.
Their mimic in elegance and dismay.

2.

She sees just what she likes in the pictures.

He brushes an ash from his cheek.

All it all comes down to
Is a simple little show of affection
Affected for you in the tables and spoons but
Sensible to the utmost
Limits of impertinence.

Your only answer
A flash of your arms.
A sudden swirl
Across the crowded dancefloor
Of ticket-stubs and coasters,
Feet amassed as a kind of blaze
Or blur might be
Scissored in to the accompaniment.

3.

Here I try in my own way to be patient with days making their demands on me in an unhealthy spirit of hustle-bustle gung-ho exceptional clarity of intent. Tasting and almost savoring with undue pleasure and alarm these days of repeatedly re-heated coffee and cigarettes. An aesthetically motivated last-ditch grip on things that soon falls flat on its face, hopefully at the feet of subsequent opportunities.

I am trying, too, to finish some stitches that will later be a border protecting the warp-ends but the truth is: I'm lazy. I haven't really worked on it in weeks. I mention this not as a rejoinder, but to explain that rather than working at the loom I've been fingering the needles, testing the tension, smoothing canoe-shaped wooden shuttles over the fleshy part of my palm and listening to you, two or three rooms away, and that this is enough.

4.

Through boiling soup and erratically-timed obscene
phone calls I hear and see things like: Charlie
Chaplin's dog, or Big Chin and Little Chin, conferring
on the next door porch. This is a part of our ongoing
attraction. Not to mention summer always seems to
drag it all out in the streets.

"Hi, Billy Boy…how old are you?

Autumn's new sneakers in New York.

And how many times to look back?
And how many times to make a path?
And how many times to turn
Like a dancer turns
Turning away from or
Back to you.

5.
That these lapses came
To mean something harsh and particular
Is testament enough to the cadence of days
Silhouetting themselves in our images
When I say we saw ourselves there
With few regrets.
Almost unfastened.
Or that this came to me in shards
Of filling-stations and backstops
As a map might be remembered
By its likeness to a face or leaf
Or kitchen utensil

In the whole uncatalogued assembly
Of their sharply divergent views,
Ushering in an era of gaiety and bravado
Watched only by the shimmer of constant rehearsals
And the endlessly sensual distractions
So pleasing to our remembered path
Through the crabgrass, and out into the light of today.
A shimmer and a cadence which
In this peculiar climate of manufacturing jargon,
"Personal life," lickety-split admission,
Made me see their movements of once
Not as a principle of random direction
But the smoothly clenching fist of
Reason enough to be still.

6.

Everything I do or say for you.
The flowers which can now be folded
Into compact banquets, which
Flower when touched or named.

Various scenes and scenarios
Fit as neatly as cup in saucer
Into a "setting" where the sun slides down
As if the sky were folding its hands in its lap
To tell a story.

Crisp linen sleeves raised
At that exact angle
In the contained light.
A room
The perfect shambles of a companion.
To quicken or cradle sensations of drift.

Then your eyes are the converse
Of a sail in the sky.

And wind is hitting the windows again.

from Boys Will Be Boys
(B/W Press, 1980)

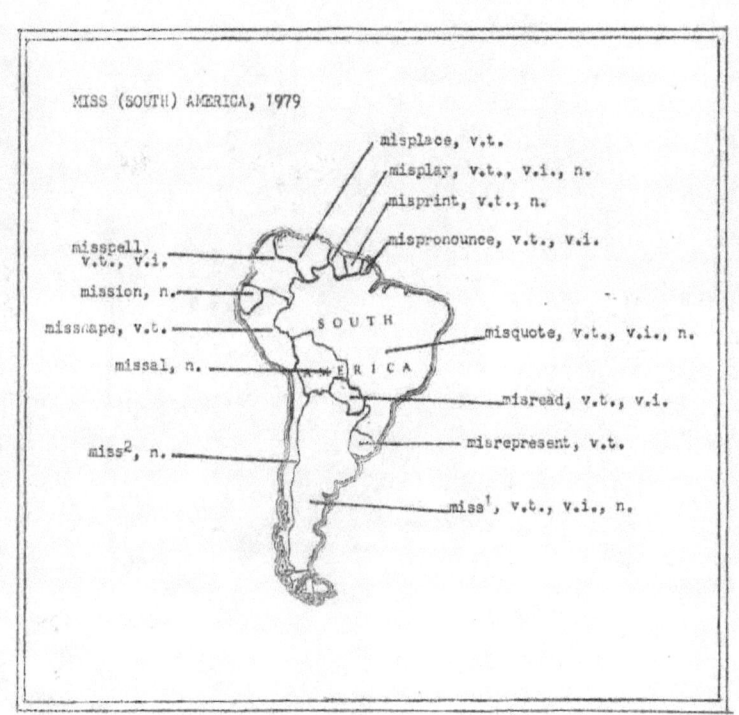

Phrase Book

If you please of course
is <u>por favor.</u>
If you say <u>gracias</u>
you are likely to hear
it's not important.
If you don't understand
say why.
Or what?
Or would you repeat that?
If you say please of course.
<u>Por favor.</u>
If you say gracias
you are likely to hear.
It's not important.
If you don't understand
say why. Or what.
Or would you repeat that.
If someone will not leave you alone
say leave me alone.
Or stop bothering me.
Or cut it out.

My Advice Is

So what? If you walk in stuttering some skeleton
geography and they all mistake it for a past? That's
what I mean about <u>style</u> and how to maintain it virtu-
ally in any situation. If it's mirrors they're after,
just bleed, but be willing to wait. My favorites are
"women" and "New York," so I sit it out here in the
mountains not entirely unwillingly inventing
this memory as I go along, the endless example of pertinent
particulars as I am always blinded to but believe.

Now when I say "believe" you should understand an
acceleration of rate of absorption vis those dimensions
by which I locate myself in the available instant, or,
should I say, <u>every</u> available instant, so that the
distance between me and my newfound home for just a
moment strikes a note (as far as you're concerned) of
inevitability, and really I'm too busy to keep count.
I know we can't argue like this much longer, lost you
said, clutching a sudden delight. But lost in a way
that lets the body bristle, adapting itself to new
situations quick enough to be recognized and
hard enough to be touched.

An ocean of panic slowly slid below the door toward
its eventual Massachusetts. And it was funny, how the
sky kept trying on those dresses it never seemed to
want to try on before. Places get scrambled. Faces do
too. There's always another place to turn to. We made
so many mistakes we called them experience, but doesn't
it sooner or later resume a logic of its own, almost
geologically, or without the more fashionable accouter-
ments? I believe that it will.

Now when I say "believe" you should understand.

One of Those Modern Angels

Who believe me
I would introduce to you in a second
Lifetime maybe, but this time it's
Try to be practical
And all you get is gossip
Reduced to a powdered blur.

It's "30 seconds over Tokyo"
Oblong on a formerly well-to-do corona
Set against your mimic of an astonished throat
By the tongues of a stopgap tide.

And to think
This innovation in desire
Had just shown itself up
In time to be recognized.
Now we were supposed to be free.

"I don't pick friends
By the color of their shoes" she said.

Later he said
"Not that you asked."

Trading a Blind Horse (Part 2)

I'm not talkin about the way she does her hair.
I'm not talkin about hydrangeas hanging from her
　white windowframes.
I'm not talkin about her doin her nails up in blue.
I'm not talkin about her underneath a beautiful tree
　say a "weeping willow" for instance.
I'm not talkin about dogs barkin by the back door.
I'm not talkin about the department-store mannequin
　she dresses like sometimes don't get me wrong.
I'm not talkin about being inseparable.
I'm not talkin about objects in or out of this room
　or any other room let alone her room.
I'm not talkin about her shadow as it moves down the
　street the way she does.
I'm not talkin about what she's always talkin about
　in her sleep.
I'm not talkin about some smell of hers.
I'm not talkin about her lips.
I'm not talkin about her as if she was a bird.
I'm not talkin about how sick she can get.
I'm not talkin about her dying.
I'm not talkin about her when she gets crazy.
I'm not talkin about her getting kidnapped.
I'm not talkin about how she'll be remembered.
I'm not talkin about lookin in the water that day and
　seeing the reflection of her face.
I'm not talkin about the woman in that photograph.
I'm not talkin about her protection.
I'm not talkin about her infections.
I'm not talkin about her bleeding.
I'm not talkin about those bloodshot half-shut eyes.
I'm not talkin about her tables of multiplication.

I'm not talkin about her transmitters.
I'm not talkin about her heroes.
I'm not talkin about her breath on her fingers or the
  window or the table or the streets or in her sleep.
I'm not talkin about her mistletoe.
I'm not talkin about her birthday cakes.
I'm not talkin about her party lights.
I'm not talkin about some image you have of her.

Parallel

A a a a a a actually afternoon amplitude are awry.
Backwards behind bristles button. Calyso-ed careless
chain checking clocks clotting cold combing cradled
cup curls curtains. Different direction disappointment
dots down drum drums. Erase escapade even eyelashes.
False finger flickers following forward. Garden. Half-
hand. Ice in in in in initially it it it its its its.
Key. Lakeside life lifting light light like lit.
Momentum mountains move my my. Need no not not not
Not numbers. Of one one out out out own. Pages pre-
scription. Reasons remark right room room. Scratched
setting smoke snow step sunlight. Tell telephone to tone
towards travelling two. Voice. Whistling windows windows
working working, You...

Checking the numbers, windows half-lit, telephone bristles,
escapade. Room remains. Initially the disappointment, the
momentum on its own, need not intrude, actually, even its
prescriptions are, following pages, a room with a view
towards forward. Setting it up again, out on a limb, work-
ing it out, working it down, messages clotting, one false
move, my cup in my hand, key chain, erase button, whistling
backwards, light surprised, curtains behind windows, ice.
A clarity of travelling, careless remark, snow-scratched
garden life-like. Sunlight flutter. Curls cradled in smoke.
Amplitude in mountains suddenly awry, combing them out,
different reasons, cold afternoon, two tone, light dots,
not trying to tell you, not lifting a finger, echo calyso-ed.
Voice flickers. Drums drum. No clocks. Eyelashes, lakeside,

a step in the right direction...

Translations

Francis Ponge

Translated by Bill Davis

La Barque

The boat pulls at the tether, moving its weight from one foot to the other, anxious and stubborn as a young horse.

Still, it's nothing but a rather coarse receptacle, a wooden spoon without a handle; but, hollowed out and curved to allow the pilot to navigate, it seems to have its own ideas, like a hand waving indifferently.

When mounted, it assumes a passive attitude, knuckles under, and is easy to lead. If it rears up, it has good reason to.

Unbridled, and left on its own, it follows the current and goes, like all the world, to its ruin, like a straw.

1976

Le Magnolia

The flower of the magnolia explodes in slow motion, like a bubble formed slowly on the thick inner wall in a syrup that's spun into caramel.

(Notice, too, the caramelized color of the leaves of this tree....)

At its full bloom, it is a heaping measure of satisfaction, proportioned to the weighty vegetal mass which in this way expresses itself.

But it isn't sticky: instead it's fresh and satiny, so much so that the leaf seems to be shining, bronzed, dry, crisp.

1976

The Cigarette

Let us first restore the atmosphere, at the time hazy and dry, disheveled, in which the cigarette is held obliquely, from the moment she has continually   been creating it forward.

Then her self: a small torch, much less luminous, less perfumed, from which detach and fall, according to a rhythm which can be ascertained, a calculable number of small masses of ash.

1976

Gérard de Nerval
from Les Chimères

Translated, with an introduction, by Bill Davis

Naming Her

"Come back," he cries.

And then in the silence the cry is consumed, the longing suppressed, illegible. Not only how she has been lost, or the names he names her with, but how in the movement or the poem she is found moving forward, image upon image, namelessly, and then how easily the ringdoves lift away. The dancer's hands shape a pair of wings in the fabric that then take up the dance themselves, so easily—the sadness barely surfaces before it is borne away.

The sapphire, azure, purple, white, and rose erase themselves, to be absorbed back into the light of the sun: It is an arc, a chromatic motion of arching, back to the Mother-star. And by this passage passion forgets itself, the shapes it suffers and the images it bears, forgets itself to fly, unroll, and overflow, and float, and then to be found becalmed with her, awaiting that light from the east.

It is a dance with a dream.

•

Her movement, dispersed in music, is almost subversive, almost obscures the poet in the poem. The vague, melancholic landscapes gently tease the ear and eye. The images give themselves over whole.

This is no drunkenness, no dulling of the senses, but a lullaby, leading us by the ear through the heart and heat of the poem, bearing us across the lull that separates its images in song. It is a calming, "to bring into a specified condition by soothing and reassuring." A lullaby is *une berceuse,* a song for the cradle or bed, forming a melodic architecture under the arch of *les berceaus,* the branches in the arbor, from which we swing in her sweet voice.

•

What "sense" the sonnet informs in us is that gathering of images we realize in the wake of their appearance on a vocal surface that offers no real resistance. The column of sapphire leads, turn by turn, to the cold gate, one moment of rest transformed into another, as if nothing had changed, as if nothing mattered but to wait there for what has been sleeping, enclosed, encoded, and might yet rise.

The first few lines evoke the motion of the dancer's headband as the purples unroll, and following her through the poem, loosening her armor, discarding her veils, she becomes the priestess, whom Nerval identifies in a note on the manuscript as "Amany." She is a character Nerval recalls from the ballet *Les Colombes (The Doves)*, performed for a small circle of friends in Paris in 1838. This memory is so sweet he implores her to return, and asks that if she see Benares, she loosen her armor and put down her bow.

Benares is in turn the signal of what will come, at a distance, accessible to the poem only through the memory of the dancer the poem recalls. Benares, in another annotation, is "the daughter of Mars." But where Mars was a noble, masculine, Roman god, who punished enemies and whose chariot was preceeded by discord, this daughter's name retains the Greek Ares, who fathered Eros, whose symbols were the burning lamp, the spear, and the vulture. She appears to be the oracle of harmony, her name itself a conjunction of Arabic and Greek, the seed of that elusive union of West and East, of persevering love that blooms in the wake of her father's chariot.

•

The poet enters the poem: "For I am the Vulture, flying over the Patani." This is no longer simply a nostalgia whose imagery is intended to be made more personal by whatever succeeding images the reader might uncover in herself. Instead, the flight of the vulture is a malevolent vortex where the desperation and desire are made visible and irrevocable by the sudden, predatory intrusion of Nerval.

This appearance seems awkward, discomforting. Nerval was recalled by his friends as a tender and humble man, even in the depths of his obsessions. So the disjunction between the poet's intrusion and the images he recalls cannot be dismissed as a marginal lapse or flaw, but rather central to the poem's power. Nor are these images mere illusions he would conjure up, but, as nearly as they can be named, the exact forms and terms of the illusions he was prey to, *les chimeres*. Yet the inclusion of the first person singular is not possible without some compensating loss in the dream's dance: recognition only diminishes its transparence and allure.

Nerval, translating Jean-Paul Richter: "<u>Je veux t'enlever tes filles, Eve. Je rassemblerai tes papillons blancs sur la fange des marais.</u>" I want to lift up your daughters, Eve. I will gather your white butterflies from the mud of the swamps.

•

The poem's title and dedication refer to Carmen Aguado, whose eldest son, Jean-Manuel, had been Nerval's host during a journey through Europe in 1839. This son, Nerval remarked, had not only his father's passion and intelligence, but the mother's grace and charm as well. His friendship with the family was intermittent but strong. When Monsieur Aguado died in April of 1842, far from home, Nerval was apparently so moved by Madame Aguado's placid and courageous mourning that the poem was written as an epistle of both sympathy and admiration.

The odd conjunction of the poem's dedication and Nerval's appearance as the vulture, as well as the more hidden, occulted intentions of the poem, can probably be traced to a coincident tragedy, the death in June of the same year of Jenny Colon. She, the critics and biographers would claim, became for Nerval, the elusive incarnation of all the women he had ever dreamed of. His mother, who he never knew. The woman he wed (in play) in the woods of the Valois and never saw again. The goddesses of the poems. The perfect lover who always would escape him, this time into death.

The poem was probably written in 1842, and presumes to offer the understanding and companionship which can only be extended from the widower to the widowed. It was not published, however, until 1924, and then from a privately owned manuscript, so it is not known if the poem was ever delivered.

•

Nerval to Theo Gautier from the Ghildaz Hotel in Constantinople, 1843: "I have lost, kingdom by kingdom, province by province, the more beautiful half of the universe, and soon I shall no longer know where to give refuge to my dreams."

•

A second manuscript, belonging to the poet Paul Eluard, was subsequently published, and it contains two of the later sonnets in the sequence *Les Chimeres* and an alternative version of "A Madame Aguado" entitled "Erythrea." If 1842 seems the likely date "A Madame Aguado" was written, the sonnets which accompany "Erythrea" indicate a much later time, 1851 or 1852. It was apparently a poem Nerval kept returning to, finally discarding it in 1853 when he felt compelled to publish *Les Chimeres*. "Delfica," one of the pieces in that sequence, duplicates (with one significant variation) the final tercet of "Erythrea," so one of the poems was destined to be secondary, to be the unsatisfactory alternative.

In comparing "Erythrea" with the earlier "A Madame Aguado," it seems that with the very simple substitutions and alterations Nerval has made of the same images a much less troubled poem of more explicit and expansive scope. If the earlier poem conveyed mourning and sympathy, "Erythrea" envisions a reunion that has not yet been realized. It is a quiet plea for constancy and patience, itself a witness to the agencies of transformation hope is embodied by.

•

In several places Nerval has simply underlined words, a practice he came to in writing *Les Chimeres* that was intended to indicate and emphasize the powers made manifest to him in various objects and beings. So the Column of Sapphire is more clearly personified, Benares' oracular appearance more assured. Nerval is no longer himself the vulture but now simply testifies to its flight, as well as that of the white butterflies. The Arc of the Sun rises from the poem more conspicuously near the close. And where in the first poem the doves took wing from their nest, here they are weeping and searching. No longer does the poet advise the loosening of the dancer's corset, but urges her, instead, to take up her bow, to fasten the stays of her breastplate.

The one invoked in the first tercet is no longer Lanassa, but Mahdewa, though they have a certain geographical relationship. The only apparent sources for the name Lanassa are a small island in the Persian Gulf, Ahassa or Lhassa (an island which protects the Queen of Saba) or Lhassa, the holy city of Tibet, which lies northwest of Patani and north of the city Benares in the Ganges valley. Mahdewa is an apparent hybrid of Nerval's scholarship, imagination, and confusion, a curiously feminized form of Mahadoeh, one of the alternate names of the masculine Hindu deity Shiva.

Shiva, of course, is the one who dances. Whose dance is the onset of chaos in the endless cycle of the universe's death and rebirth, the destruction of the old order, the death of the old ways. Shiva contrasts in particular with Vishnu, who rules the age of calm that follows the dance. Vishnu is pictured being carried by a bird—sometimes an eagle, sometimes a vulture, across a sea of silk.

•

The Snow of Cathay

Still the Priestess—who in the Tarot dreams of becoming God—is sleeping, awaiting the return of her beloved throughout the harsh rule of the priest. She has prepared herself for the coming eclipse and herself defends the true light. In a variation of these lines in "Delfica," Nerval has the priestess of a Latin countenance, sleeping below the Arch of Constantine, which he visited during his trip to Virgil's grave at Posilipo. It was here Constantine swore that the Muslims, the orientals, the pagans, would never pass.

•

What, or who, are we waiting for, when nothing has shaken this cold gate? To look her whole in the face and still speak, to speak in a language these images envision that was never really lost, if only because possessing it was another, older illusion, another dream, whose accumulated names overflow. Nerval writes, "the illusions peel away, like the skin of a fruit, and the fruit is <u>experience</u>."

Michelangelo has painted the Erythrean sibyl on the ceiling of the Sistine Chapel, where she seems as calm and relaxed as the Delphic oracle is excited. She sits quietly, contemplating a large book. One of her attendants holds a lamp for her. The other rubs his eyes sleepily.

So, she is *Erythrea,* the sibyl, the prophetess, author of oracles on the passion of Christ, the downfall of Rome, and author, too, of a long poem which foretells the final judgment.

She is *Erythras,* and the Red Sea—the Erythrean Sea—takes its name from her victims: Erythras is the Sanskrit equivalent of the Hindu Roudhiras, whose name means *the red one, the bloody one.* Roudhiras is the storm of destruction that initiates Shiva's dance.

She is the dancer, or the dance—the one who, like Shiva, will release the breath of the world, the breath of mortals, and the breath of gods, back into chaos and formlessness, to take new forms, to find new images, to be reborn, to awaken.

A Madame Aguado

Column of sapphire, embroidered arabesque,
Come back. A ring of doves takes wing from the nest.
From your azure headband to your granite feet,
Unrolling in pleats, are all the purples of Judea.

If you see Benares, leaning on her river,
Loosen with your bow your burnt-golden stays,
For I am the Vulture flying over Patani
And white butterflies overflow the sea.

Lanassa, float your veil across these waters,
Deliver the purple flowers to the whispering streams.
The snow of Cathay falls on the Atlantic,

Still the priestess with the rose-colored skin
Is sleeping under the arc of the sun,
And nothing has shaken the cold gate.

El Desdichado

I am the darkness—the widower—the unconsoled,
The Prince of Aquitaine at the broken tower:
My only <u>Star</u> is dead—and my constellated lute
Bears the <u>Black Sun</u> of melancholy.

In the night of the tomb, you who consoled me,
Give me back Posilipo and the sea of Italy,
The <u>flower</u> so pleasing to my desolate heart,
The trellis where the vine-branch is one with the rose.

Am I Amor or Phoebus? Lusignon or Biron?
My forehead is still red with the Queen's kiss.
I have dreamed in the grotto where the siren swims.

And twice I have crossed the Acheron, unvanquished,
Mingling on the lyre of Orpheus, turn by turn,
The cries of a fairy and a saint.

Myrtho

I think of you Myrtho, divine enchantress,
Of proud Posilipo, brilliant with a million fires,
Of your forehead overflowing with the lights of the Orient,
Of black grapes woven with the gold of your hair.

It was from your cup I drank this drunkenness
And from the secret light of your delighted eye
When you saw me praying at the feet of Iacchus,
For the muse had made me one of the sons of Greece.

I knew why the volcano there re-opened.
Because yesterday you touched it with your quick feet
And its ashes now cover the horizon.

Because a Norman duke has broken your clay gods
And forever beneath the laurel branch of Virgil,
The pale hydrangea merges with the green myrtle.

Delfica

Daphne, do you know this old romance?
At the foot of the sycamores, below the white branches,
Under the olives or myrtle or the trembling willows,
This love song always beginning again?

Do you remember the TEMPLE, with its immense columns,
And the bitter lemons in which you pressed your teeth?
Or the fatal cave of the shameless hosts
Where the old dragon's seed is sleeping?

Those gods you keep crying for will come back,
Time will restore the old order.
The earth has trembled with a prophetic sigh.

Still the sibyl with the Latin silhouette
Is sleeping under the Arch of Constantine
--and nothing has shaken the cold gate.

Horus

The god Kneph, trembling, shook the universe.
Then Isis, the mother, rose from her bed.
She made a gesture of hatred at her savage husband
And the old fires shone in her green eyes.

"Look at him," she said. "The old pervert is dying.
All the frost of the world has passed through his mouth.
Bind up his crooked feet. Put out his cloudy eye.
He is the god of the volcanoes and the king of winter.

The eagle has already passed. The new spirit calls me.
I have put on the robe of Cybele for him again.
He is the child beloved of Hermes and Osiris."

Then the goddess fled on her golden shell
But the sea repeated her sweet image for us,
And the skies flamed below the scarf of Iris.

Vers Dores

You "free thinker" you—do you really think alone
In this world where the mind in everything explodes?
Your freedom arranges these powers you hold on to
But who in the universe will miss your advice?

Notice: in the animal, a spirit stirs.
Each flower in nature has its own soul to bloom.
A mystery of love smolders even in steel.
All of them: sensible, and with their power over you.

Beware of the blind walls who have their eye on you.
A verb is attached even to matter
But don't make it serve some petty usage.

Often in the unintelligible the genius is concealed.
And like an embryonic eye still sealed in its lids
A pure spirit grows below the skin of the stones.

Artemis

The thirteenth returns. Her again, the first one.
She is still the only one or: this is the only moment.
But are you the Queen? Are you the first or the last?
Are you the King? Are you the only or only the latest lover?

Love whoever loved you from the cradle to the grave.
The only one I ever loved still loves me tenderly.
She is Death. Or: The Dead One. My torment and delight.
The rose she holds is the <u>rose-tremiere</u>.

You, Saint of Naples, with your hands full of fire,
Rose with a violet heart, flower of St, Gudule.
Did you find your crossroad in the deserted skies?

Those white roses will have to fall. You ridicule our gods.
Those white phantoms will fall from your sky through the flames.
The saint of the abyss is holier in my eyes.

from You Can See That It's Just The Walls That Are Standing (Just Empty Walls)

Genevieve Davis (1914 - 2002),
Morales Davis (1915 - 1982)

Photos Small, 3 inches by 1 1/2 inches

These photos are small, 3 inches by 1 1/2 inches, and are all part of the same roll, although it's unclear whether they are all shot the same day or over a period of days. Each one has a number on the back, but only #3, #5 and #6 are dated. On the back, in my mother's handwriting, is the inscription "Pierceport Hotel" and the date "9/18/38." It is the day after my mother and father are married, pictures of their honeymoon in the Poconos.

The hotel itself appears at first to be the subject of two photos. In one, judging from the angle of the sun and the quality of the light, the southeast corner of the hotel lies near the center of the image, slightly out of focus, and the shade of a wide, low maple falls across the eastern side of the two-story building. In the other, the focus is quite sharp, but the vantage point very different, perhaps on the opposite side of the building. After awhile, though, I realize that it is a similar but different building, for none of the architectural details in the two views can quite be united into a single structure in my mind's eye. This takes some time to determine, though, as one's attention is elsewhere in the second photograph, for its focal point is a large, uprooted tree which lies between the camera and the building in the middle distance, damage from the Hurricane of '38.

There are eight prints, equally divided, of my mother and father in bed. The ones of my father are badly blurred. In one, he lays in bed with the covers up to his chest, his arms above his head as if stretching when first awakening, though the scene has a quality of being deliberately posed. Sunlight falls across the bed. My father is smiling. In another photograph of him, one arm lays on the pillow above his head and again he smiles broadly. In this one, too, he is blurry. He may have been moving, but I think it is more likely that my mother moves as she took the picture, or that, even with the sunlight falling through the wooden shutters, there isn't quite enough light and the shutter opens and closes more slowly than she expects or is accustomed to.

The photographs of my mother are sharp. In one, she is at the extreme bottom of the frame. Whereas my father's gaze swept towards the foot of the bed, propelled by his wide smile, my mother is almost prone and peeks demurely over the covers, which are up around her shoulders. In another, soft fists lie atop the blankets, and although her expression is never completely readable, she seems to have an understated, closed-lip smile as she peers down over the bed towards the camera. On the wall above the bed is a painting of two silhouetted sailing ships, one in the middle distance, one much further away.

In each of these photos of them in bed, but especially in the ones of my father, there are clouds or whorls of light, cirrus-like swirls spread across the images, in and out of the pale sunlight, across the bed, surrounding the figures with a haze of brightness, the brownish tint of all the pale objects faintly brushed with an additional wash that has begun to obscure them. My mother and father, wrapped in this sepia gauze, partially hidden by these thin, delicate clouds, appear themselves to be made of watery brown light, are wrapped in a swirl of visible air the color of earth mixed with water.

I wonder, as I study these photographs, if these small nebulae have always been there, or if they appear gradually as the photographs age. Wonder, too, what my mother and father say to each other when they first see them, first see themselves married, in bed. Wonder what they say to each other as the photographs are taken, or if they show them to anyone else, or how often they take them out to look at, or when they stop. There is no way to know. Too much happens, between the years that pass and all the losses that add and remove meanings. Language changes, too, over so long a time, even language for that which is most precious to us, most loved, most familiar, and after a certain time cannot be trusted, for anticipation, regret or desire can all coalesce and fade, as events recede behind the clouds of other events, and the language that may have given a scene life, at first gradually, and later more quickly, diminishes, is lost, leaving just these mute, ghost-images, suffused with artifacts of light.

There is one stray photograph of my mother. She is sitting on one side of a double-seated swing that has slatted benches for two on either side of a small platform, the entire structure hanging from four long struts. My mother looks at the camera while she sits at the near end of one of the benches. She is wearing a bandana, a jacket over what looks like a white sweater or blouse, a skirt, socks and loafers. It is hard to read her expression. Some leaves are on the ground. On the back, marked in pencil, is the number 37. On the left side of the photo, there is a vertical bar of light, as if the glare from some object has caused an area of the film to be overexposed, though this area is 1/2-inch in from (and parallel to) the left-hand border of the photo, and enough around this area can be seen to determine that the area is not aligned with any object, and instead appears to be the kind of blemish that often appears on the last frame in a roll, which in this case was for 36 exposures. This is the "extra" image that is often available, and must be taken in order to finish the roll, even if it is impossible to know at the time how it will come out.

A flattened bay the color of brushed steel or, where it is entirely sheltered from the mid- November breeze, slate oiled and polished until it gleams in the icy sunlight, a geometric membrane of gray stretched between the mainland and the point. Extending several hundred feet offshore, beginning further up the small stream beneath this bridge, there is a crescent of soft ice the shape of the moon. When the moon is full now, the moonlight falls through the porch windows before dawn, lays like a ghost on the floor. By Tuesday, it will be gone. This is the sheltered dip in the road where twice I've seen a doe cross, once in the fall, moving away from the bay, and now. This time, we're both moving in the opposite direction. I'm on my way back, going home.

Photograph Number *182*

The figures in this photograph are nowhere identified, and I am surprised, really, by how many photos have, in my mother's upward-looping, right-leaning handwriting (which I see sometimes reflected in my own) a simple listing of those pictured. Sometimes, on older photographs, like this one, a woman's maiden name may also be given, usually in parentheses. Sometimes, too, a year is given, sometimes a location, sometimes names and a year and a location, fixing all the essentials.

This photograph has none, just the number **182**, diagonally written in one quadrant on the reverse side. Held up to the light, it is scrawled directly across the three people in the photograph - the woman, the boy and the little girl. The boy is wearing a cap, a coat, knickers, knee socks and shoes, and leans on some kind of stick or mallet. The girl has a wide, dark hat, a coat, white socks, and carries a basket in her right hand while holding in front of her, with her left, what appears to be a lollipop. The woman has a long skirt, dark jacket and fur hat. Behind them, at some distance, two buildings meet as they recede, defining a foreshortened disappearing point just behind the woman, with low trees across the juncture of the buildings.

It is the buildings, I decide later - one four stories high, of glass and cement, the other lower by one story, longer looking, also glass and cement, resembling a postwar junior high school - that postpone for so long my realization that the photo is much older than I thought, delay my recognition of my mother (the girl), her brother Wes and their mother, who died when I was six. My mother's father, absent from the photo, presumably because he stood on this side of the camera, came to live with us then, in Queens, and died there during the night, I can't quite remember, either on New Year's Eve or the day before New Year's Eve, 1960, four years later.

My mother is squinting and her brother has his head cocked and slightly turned away, while their mother looks straight ahead, fierce, proud, aware, it seems, that her image will be captured and attending closely to her portion of that task, even if preparing properly then renders her momentarily sun-blind. Long after she is gone, she continues to look directly and clearly at the viewer, withstands whatever scrutiny is brought to the meaning or character of this otherwise casual and ordinary snapshot.

My mother now is legally blind in both eyes. Her mother died 41 years ago, her brother 22 years ago. By now, this photograph is almost 80 years old, and, much as I try, I can no longer reconstruct the state of mind in which the figures there were unknown, not yet my mother, not yet her brother and mother, just three people from long ago - a stately mother, oblivious to all beyond the gaze of the camera, and her children, keeping their hands at their sides, trying to shield themselves from the light.

Tables have been arranged around the perimeter of the adjoining rooms, with generous helpings of hors d'oeuvres, meatballs, breads, cakes, crackers, cheeses, fruits and cookies, and the families of many of the residents circulate, gather chairs together in small groups, chat as they fill small paper plates. I find I have to navigate several worlds: the world of our family (that is, just the four of us), of communication with the staff, of interaction with my mother, then my mother's own world and the fragmented, slippery world the residents seem to share, filled with a million little pockets of anger and shame and fear that can be at one instant bundled together at full force, and, a moment later, utterly dispersed into tiny, silent worlds that labor and struggle to persist, and can so easily be crushed by the simplest of events, worlds already nearly empty, hollow and frail, then the sound of thin plastic punch cups, cracking in the children's hands, while a man plays Christmas carols at the piano, a sweet, slightly overweight man, who plays with warmth, creating small interludes of response around the room, as people stop to sing along for a little, automatically, not even knowing if they're singing, the song transporting them momentarily to another time, then back and on again. After that things start slipping again.

By now, all the stories are shorter. Her stories. My stories about her. Some of the longer stories here already feel old. Much less changes now. Raw materials diminish, grow precious. The whole idea of a "story" seems forced, selfish, contrived. Events continue to recede into loss. Time is unforgiving, but stories are not, even when the memory at the heart of a story is displaced, populated with orphans of other stories, weighted with feelings that arose somewhere else, beyond what we can still remember we forget. There is always this ebb and flow, the flux of continuous reordering that gathers itself and spills forward. The waves are long, and sometimes pass only with a great deal of pain and difficulty until, in the sweet undertow of relief, yesterday is still there, or the memory of her mother in old age, the story about when her mother broke her ankle, the words for "snow" and "coat," several days of the week. Yes, it's Thursday alright. The radio said so. And now the stories have their own ideas about where to go. A recollection of my mother's mother at the dinner table appears to conclude now with an episode involving her brother, many years earlier, then fully dissolves into his wife's love of flowers, especially chrysanthemums, which they grow in a small greenhouse in their back yard in New Jersey.

The week after the ice storm, there is a thick gauze of snowfall dampening the scars in the fresh wood, dressing the mounds of branches, lain out in the open, not really yet quite dead. Spring snow covers them one last time. Thinning the flowers in the vase, I find even the best-looking blossoms fall apart at my touch, and only the greens remain: the tiny flowerlets and tiny gray-green leaves, Baby's Breath.

When we visit with friends of my parents', sooner or later the men are all together, in a room with a television or in a back yard by a charcoal grill, drinking and talking about the war. Where they were. What they did. Their talk is big and empty. The women gather, too, usually in a kitchen or living room, or perhaps in another part of the yard if the yard is big enough, most of them having coffee or tea, some having a drink, even if it is still just lunchtime, and talk instead of expanding circles of children and houses and schools and friends and relatives and marriages and deaths and illnesses and vacations and clothing and meals.

There is one family we see just once a year or so - friends of my parents from the old days in Brooklyn - a family that lives, with their two adopted children, in the woods of northern Connecticut. The man has not been in the service at all (though I don't know why), and he and my father talk instead of things built, planted, planned. Of jobs, cars, houses, tools, gadgets, gizmos, catalogues, parts. Their talk seems small and empty, and I wonder over and over again, even years later, as talk of the war almost disappears, replaced by other talk, by another war, what it must be like to have such vast events consume so many years of relative youth - my father is 28 when he is drafted - then have nothing of the same scale occur for the rest of one's life. Wonder if it is possible at all to recall events as they unfolded, not yet transformed by the war's sudden end, or the flight from the cities later, the children and schools and houses and jobs and cars that all accumulated over the years, inflating, nurturing, diminishing their lives.

Photographs: Silvery, Angular Tabs

There are three pages of photographs: small two-inch by three-inch prints, held in place by silvery, angular tabs pasted to the pages. BAPTIST CHURCH is a sturdy, squat stone structure, with a triangular top wall above the front door, lying fully in shadow, late in the day, facing east.

AN AMARILLO MANSION sits on a corner lot, not too far back, with no wall or fence of any kind, but pillars on a semi-circular entranceway visible through thin, bare trees lining the street.

Three photos sit in a neat triangle above the words POLK STREET METHODIST CHURCH. The first shows another brick building, also with a triangular front peak that, judging from the sunlight, faces north by northwest, almost lost in a grove of low trees across the otherwise empty city block that lies in the foreground.

The entrance is filled with people leaving the church in the second photograph. They descend a wide stone staircase with two intermediate landings on the long path down to the street.

The center of the third is completely washed out with sunlight, a ghost of the same entrance, perhaps from across the street, two sleek cars at the curb.

The POTTER COUNTY COURTHOUSE is a stone building that faces a block of relatively young, evenly spaced trees, though it's unclear why a photograph of this particular building is included.

Another, unlabeled, shows what is apparently an eleven or twelve story hotel, in shadows, in the distance, topped with the words *Santa Fe* in electric lights.

On the rounded, southwest corner of a one story deco building are the letters KGNC.

4th + POLK shows a woman crossing a street, a Model A parked beneath the trefoil globes of streetlights, two story storefronts on the opposite street and another tall hotel, four or six blocks away.

On the third page are photos of the "Auditorium USO," another brick affair, with two front towers, that might once have been a mission. One of my mother, leaning against the side of an arch at the entrance. One very blurry shot of my father, completely in shadow, in front of the arches. Another is labeled "Downtown USO," though the two-story building barely occupies the left-hand half of the image.

Two final shots are labeled "Elwood Park." One of my father, in uniform, his hands at his sides, in front of a large shrub. One of my mother and father, sitting together on a rough, flat bench in front of a tree, a picture taken by a buddy or, more likely, a passerby.

My mother falls. The night nurse calls to tell me. After deciding to not visit tonight, my first thought is that if I were there it would not have happened, although I recognize this thought as false, covering the feelings that instead go with visiting less over a period of time, creating a dramatic narrative in which to place other thoughts, other feelings, or to transform the situation into something larger, something also false.

The nurse tells me that my mother is OK, although she apparently does nothing to break the fall, and lands on her face, cutting her lip and forehead. Her glasses are not broken. Her other glasses are still lost.

The next day, the head nurse calls to tell me that my mother is alright, but has a large shiner and a large bruise around her mouth. She tells me that my mother does not remember the fall. That if someone asks how she feels or asks what happened, she does not know what they're talking about.

I go to see my mother and we go for a ride. The side of her face that is bruised - a deep, dark reddish purple - is the side I see when I turn in her direction, although it is true that she doesn't seem to have any awareness that she has been hurt or is bruised. I wonder what happens when she looks in the mirror in her bathroom and sees this face, wonder if she sees what has happened but forgets as soon as she is away from the mirror, or perhaps doesn't realize what she's seeing when she looks in the mirror, or perhaps doesn't realize she is seeing herself, or perhaps just what I think she must see, who she must see, is not seen anymore at all, is no longer there, and this image that I see, or the image she sees and then loses, cannot replace or bruise or harm the other image, set loose from time, lost now, gone, untouchable, intact.

The long loops are gone. The stories are gone. The repeating phrases are gone. The words circling around each other and the events they surround are gone. The sentences that unfold and gather themselves and immediately unfold again are gone. Now there are just sentences begun, stories suggested, loops that trail off unclosed, phrases set loose from other phrases, words invented, events unformed, sentences folded shut before they open, languages created anew from little tremors of the teeth and lips and tongue where the sentences trail off, guttural sounds replacing the parts of speech, dissolving stories into a trembling chin, the sound of vowels, consonants congested at the edge of the teeth, words useless, phrases set free, trails, circles, mouth, loops, teeth, folds, starts and stops, and will not move.

"How long have I been here?" asks my mother. It is early February. I am sitting in the rocking chair in her room, the one she and my father buy when we move in 1961. She is sitting in the reclining chair Wes and I pick out shortly before she arrives in Vermont.

"Just about exactly a year and a half," I answer.

In the basement, most of the boxes are still unpacked: crystal, napkins, desk supplies, silver serving trays, bank records, the metal doll from her childhood, small woodworking projects of my father's. The only boxes I open are the smaller ones - shoeboxes, most of them - filled with photographs and papers.

Some of these photographs and papers my mother saves and moves with her from 1757 Albany Avenue, the house she grows up in and then goes back to when the war comes and separates them, then to the place they rent after the war, then to Queens, where I am born, then out on the Island and, finally, after my father dies, to Florida. As with everything else I find helping my mother prepare to move again, there is no order to these things, but they have been saved.

There is a photograph of a Mr. Gibney - my mother's mother's father - holding the reins of two horses at his stable in Brooklyn, and two of his handwritten receipts. A photograph of an unidentified woman with her hair up under a broad, lacy hat, a woman with a proud chin and high collar. A photograph of my mother's mother and father, probably in their late thirties. Papers from the high school my father attended, in Lee, Massachusetts. Pictures of my mother's father in uniform.

And my father's letters.

"That was a hard time," says my mother. "He didn't even think they'd take him in the service because his eyes were so bad. Without his glasses, he was like this." She squints her eyes, barely able now to see herself, and waves her hands and arms frantically.

"Sometimes three letters would arrive at once. Other times two weeks would go by without a letter, and I would think 'He's been shot.' My mother would get so mad at me. 'Why do you have to think the worst?' she would ask. But it was a very hard time. Oh, and it seems so long ago now."

She looks around her room. "And I never dreamed I'd end up here."

It is dark outside.

"But that was a hard time," she says, after a long pause. "I wouldn't ever want to live through that again."

When my father is inducted in 1943, he is tested and evaluated for various skills, and it is determined that he has a great deal of aptitude in cryptography. He receives training in this area. The only practical application he ever has for this training, however, is to devise a personal code with which he can insert hidden messages into his letters, and the document "Code Instructions - Final Edition" covers both sides of a small piece of stationery.

If a letter begins "Geney Darling," it is *not* a letter with a coded message. The key letters are the second letters following a dash, which he uses liberally. Occasionally, messages are split between letters, and the number of times the phrase "I love you" appears indicates which portion of the message is in a given letter, unless it is used as part of the phrase "I love you, kitten," in which case the entire message is in the letter. The letters - that is, the second letter following a dash - themselves are coded, and a key is included in the instructions. If the message is received, my mother is to write back "Everything is OK at home," whereas if the message is not received successfully, she will say something about "Lucy," which is her mother's name.

Our mail will be censored, he writes, *from the time we step on the troop train until the time we return to the US from our tour overseas.*

I imagine it takes my mother longer to decode these simple messages than it takes to read the letters, and in June of 1945, when they finally part, she has written the first few messages on the front of the envelopes: "Stuffing a duffle bag," "Viewing Salt Lake," "We're On Our Way," "Coconut Grove." The subsequent letters, however, from June 25 on, all bear the stamp of an Army Examiner in the place on the face of the envelope where my mother had been writing the coded messages, which now appear on the back - "Crossing the Pacific," "Sailing, Sailing," "Manila to Leyte," "Going Across," "My Trip Over."

My father tells me to do something. I am small.

"Why?" I say.

"In the army," says my father, "they don't tell you why."

July 29, 1945
In the Philippines
Rec'd August 6, 1945

At last we landed – Boy it sure was good to set foot on solid earth again. We landed in Manila yesterday noon. We were originally scheduled to land two days sooner at another place, but evidently there was a last minute change in plans.

The trip was really much better all around than I thought it would be. But the novelty wore off after the first week and from there on it was the same day after day. We passed quite a few places where history was made during this war. The voyage was interesting but it was just too far between stops and just too much water for me.

Manila, even though I believe it has been cleaned up considerably, still shows the ravages of war. There are lots of sunken ships in the harbor – you can see the tops of them sticking up above the water here and there. Several buildings have been completely wrecked. Others have cannon holes in them and there are lots that have bullet holes in the walls. Some are just holes from rifle shots but here and there you can see some that have been sprayed with machine gun bullets. Along the roads and in the open lots there are several wrecked Jap planes of various kinds. All around the camp here there are various pieces of Jap equipment as decorations in front of headquarters buildings and orderly rooms.

The natives line up outside the camp every day selling bananas, coconuts and pineapples. Everything – no matter what you buy – costs one peso, about fifty cents. They really do a business, too. What amuses me though is that we can trade them a pack of cigarettes for any item that costs one peso and the cigarettes cost us five cents. Some of them are very fussy about what brand of cigarettes they take in trade too – nothing but the most popular brands.

They're not allowed to come into the camp to sell things until after 4 o'clock in the afternoon. They wait outside until the dot of four and then they come in in droves. The majority of ones that come through selling things are young girls and very young boys. The older fellows gather under a nice shady tree while the girls are doing the selling.

This is our old "lonesomest" day here, but back there I believe it is still Saturday. There's quite a difference in time – just what it is I don't know, but it makes it awfully hard for me to picture what you are doing at various times. I'll have to find out somewhere just what the time difference is so I can get straightened out. As near as I can figure it is sometime Saturday night where you are, but it is 3 o'clock Sunday afternoon here.

Right now I'm trying to make up my mind whether to go into Manila or not – it looks very much like rain and I don't know whether to chance it. Last night we had a good shower and today it is muddy with a capital "M."

(Later)

I went into Manila today but didn't get a chance to do much sightseeing – as I was afraid it might do, it rained like the dickens. There are no buses into town – we just go out on the road and thumb a ride – there are all kinds of vehicles going by and they are pretty good as far as stopping for you is concerned.

Manila isn't very much to look at. I imagine that before the war it was fairly pretty in some sections. Many of the buildings look as though they were very modernistic. There are hardly any buildings untouched – they are just a mass of blasted rubble. It really is a mess. Lots of places look as though they are unmarred but when you get close to them you can see that it's just the walls that are standing – just empty walls.

Outside of looking at the terrible damage there is really nothing to see – some sections are very very poor. I did get to see Intramuros where some of the bitterest fighting took place – the walls around there are at least 20 feet thick – they blasted right through them.

My mother calls. It is hot, she says, and I don't know how lonely she is, and her best friend is gone, as of either yesterday or today, and although she promised herself she wouldn't cry if she called me she just can't help it. It's only eight o'clock and everyone has gone to bed already, there isn't a *soul* in the place and it's still daylight, and how is she supposed to live like this? She can't live like this, she says, can't take it anymore.

I have learned, after a few initial mistakes two years ago, to not even begin to talk about anything that in any way suggests, or in any fashion refers to, the complete lack of alternatives.

At least the man across the hall who fell and broke his hip is back, the man who helps her cut her food. And the woman who wouldn't look at her is gone. But now there isn't a *soul* in the hallway or the screened-in porch or the big room with the TV. And her friend left yesterday. Or maybe it was today.

October 21, 1945 Leyte

Lee and I managed to get our jeep OK. We really had a swell time – we went swimming for awhile and then went sightseeing – I don't know whether the towns we went through show on your map or not, but we went through Palo, Tanuan, Dulag and Tacloban. There were also any number of smaller villages we went through too.

While we were in Dulag we visited an old church there that was ruined when our Navy shelled the town prior to the invasion. The church was over 200 years old. They had salvaged a lot of carved wooden fixtures and ornaments, and there were several life-sized statues carved out of solid pieces of wood.

Most of the route we took was all along the beach from Tacloban to Dulag. Every once in a while we stopped along the beach to inspect some ruins of a wrecked plane – unlike Manila, most of the wrecked planes here are our own planes – up there they were all Jap planes.

But my mother's calm version of herself lies in a mailbag on a San Francisco dock, while in Kansas City his impatience is thrown on a train heading east. Their messages cross, are reordered, the narratives made false by the narratives of their arrival, by events taking their exchange and restructuring it, very slowly, over several weeks, recreating itself as if it were the first time all over again and we can just keep doing this until we get it right.

And suddenly, with a dozen or more letters in transit, the war ends.

Everyone is just "sweating it out," sightseeing, driving by skeletons of planes on a beach, smelling the fish market, going to parties, the more mortal dangers giving way quickly to boredom, liquor, paperwork, shopping, monsoons, women, routine. My father longs for the day when things will be the way they were before the war – the war that, even in victory, he calls *senseless* – and they can resume what they had begun. For my mother, her biggest wish so far in her life has been fulfilled. For my father, who never really saw the war, but saw what it left as it dragged its tail away through the mud and rubble of Tacloban and Palo and Tanuan and Dulag, the wishes and worries from now on are smaller.

My father dies 36 years later - 18 years ago. He is buried in a veteran's cemetery on Long Island. I have papers that indicate the location of the grave. The only time I am there is the day he is buried. I don't know if my mother goes there again before she moves, the year after he dies. There is a place there reserved for her – I have the paperwork – but a few years after moving to Florida, she takes out a burial plot there, then changes plans twice more until, finally, sometime in the last four or five years, just like money and shopping and letters and making food, she stops thinking about it completely.

"Billy"

I.

Near our house in Queens is an area that occupies 6 city blocks - woods near the dead-end street around the corner, just off 143rd Avenue, then a swamp that runs all the way down to Springfield Boulevard and up past where Auntie Mil lives on the way to school. A creek runs under the road about halfway to Springfield Boulevard. One day there is a drowned cat floating there. Another day, nearby, there is a small cave made by some bulldozed trees and undergrowth where we gather and pretend to be soldiers. Many people in the neighborhood leave trash in the woods or swamp. In the cave, we store an Army *Field Manual* that someone finds. We have a small raft to make our way through the swamp.

On the side with the woods, there is a semi-circular path than can be travelled by bicycle, starting by Richie Tchaikovsky's house, and re-entering the dead-end street near the far end. We play war a lot, but the Japs are always imaginary. No one wants to be the Japs. We sing *Whistle while you work, Hitler was a jerk, Mussolini bit his weenie, Now it doesn't squirt*.

One day, we find a box of papers and junk, and looking through the junk, I find a small white pin with some German words on it and a red swastika in the middle. We all agree immediately on what this means: an escaped Nazi war criminal is living in the neighborhood secretly, and for a long time, we try to identify him. We have our suspicions, but are never quite successful.

Finally, I learn that the words on the pin say something like kindergarten, and someone, not my father - I don't show it to him - explains that it was probably a pin worn by children in Germany, and that it was probably a little souvenir kept by someone who finally decides to throw out all the stuff he brings home from the war. I wonder: what happened to the child who had worn the pin? How hold would she be now?

II.

I love war movies, and my father loves taking me to war movies. Usually, all three of us go. Sometimes we have dinner out - nothing fancy. I especially like the submarine movies - Burt Lancaster and Jack Warden at war with obsessive Clark Gable inside a submarine in *Run Silent, Run Deep,* or *Up Periscope* with James Garner and Edmund O'Brien. And I love *Sink the Bismarck* and buy the 45 of the theme song by Johnny Horton, his follow-up to "The Battle of New Orleans." *In May of 1941/ The war had just begun / The Germans had the biggest ships / That had the biggest guns.* I see Hollywood war movies from the 1940's on Saturday afternoons, or on *Million Dollar Movie,* which runs the same movie several times a day for a whole week.

I read *Sgt. Rock* and *Sad Sack* and *Beetle Bailey* comic books and, later, novels about the war. There is a book whose name I cannot recall that utterly sustains me through one of our summer vacations in New Hampshire, a book from the town library that involves submarine warfare, and attracts me more than anything except the book about a dog I borrow on a snowy day in third grade and never finish and never find again.

I have many toy soldiers - a few metal ones, but most of them plastic, and trucks and artillery and tanks. I especially like big "sets" of soldiers, and it is important that all of the toys involved in some scene are of the same scale. I like the smaller ones, because it's easier to get lots of them, and with lots of them I build large battle scenes that occupy the geography of our living room or back yard. In the living room, I use blocks to make buildings and walls, and lay on my side with my eyes as close to the rug as possible to see what it looks like at ground level – the snipers behind the walls, the tanks sitting between the broken buildings, the loose slabs in the middle of the battlefield.

I collect stamps with WWII battle scenes on them.

I keep the ribbons and patches from my father's army uniform in a special box and his uniform hangs, in a plastic bag, in the spare closet in my room. Once or twice, when we go into New York City, we go to a restaurant owned by Eisenhower's personal chef.

I build Revell models of aircraft carriers, tanks, destroyers, submarines, amphibious landing vehicles, B-52's, battleships, a GI in full combat gear. I especially like, after finishing a battleship or destroyer, putting the decals on, the white numbers with the gray drop shadows that adorn the bow, the gray of the shadows darker than the gray plastic of the ship, and the little anti-aircraft guns snapped carefully into place in their round little nests, free to swivel and turn, and the little barrels of the guns on deck that are inserted through narrow slits in their housings and can be gently moved up and down.

I have a black plastic submarine that shoots two torpedoes from spring-loaded torpedo tubes in the tub.

And on Sunday nights, after the peanut butter and jelly sandwiches, after *The Twentieth Century* and after *You Asked For It!*, eating dishes of hand-packed Breyer's ice cream from the soda fountain a few blocks away, there are the dark battles and black-and-white sunrises of *Victory at Sea*.

My son and my daughter and I go for a walk down the curving, tree-lined roads, the day's first sun lighting treetops as we go. The stones sunk into the hard dirt road are gleaming wet and smooth. We pry some loose. My son sees a rabbit, standing very still, a few feet into the woods near the narrow cut for the power lines and we all watch for a little bit, but a truck comes down the road and the rabbit runs off.

Now there is an open window, a silhouetted railing, a cedar trunk and branches just emerging from silhouette, the wide, steel blue of the lake, the dark flicker of small waves in the weak southwest wind, the far shore wrapped in a light, translucent gauze, the sound of the water lapping at the rocks and, in the distance, off to the south and muffled by trees, a dull throb of vehicles, machines.

4 Photographs

1

7/30/44. My mother and Aunt Marta are sitting on the wooden steps of a house I don't know. Aunt Marta is not related by blood - she was my godmother, and my mother was her daughter's godmother - but that's how I always referred to her. Her husband was Uncle Gordon, who I liked a great deal. When this photograph was taken, Uncle Gordon was in France and my father was in the Philippines. My mother has her arm around Marta's waist and Marta's arm is around my mother's shoulders. It is very sunny and a patch of glare washes out the lower left-hand corner of the photograph, blurring the line between the border and the step on which their feet rest. They are wearing light-colored summer dresses, and the dresses and their legs all glow in the bright light as they squint and try to smile.

2

The walls are covered with wallpaper, a large, bold floral print. There is a small sidetable by the wall and, on the floor, a stack of newspapers, a pillow. Our dog, Bootsy, lies between a large stuffed hassock and a heavy, dark armchair. My mother is asleep in the armchair, nearly prone, her feet crossed and balanced at one edge of the hassock, one hand behind her and one at her mouth. It is 1958 or 1959 or 1960. The flash lights up the dog's eyes.

3

7/9/50 is written on the reverse of the photograph. My mother is sitting on the side of our front stoop. The first few numerals of our address are visible on the far right-hand side, next to the door. She is holding me up in front of her. I am 9 months old. There are many different reasons given in its retelling over the years - the *rh* blood situation, her age, what happened the other time - but as she holds me here with my feet on the stoop, the doctor has already told her she shouldn't have any more children. She holds me knowing this. My arms dangle loosely, my fingers resting on her arms. She holds me at the waist and my legs are still bowed. My face obliterates her face.

4

My mother is standing in front of a brick house in Brooklyn. Other houses, further down the street, have awnings over their windows, elaborate wrought-iron fences and railings. My mother is holding a white umbrella. She is wearing a white dress and white shoes. She is seven years old and her hair is freshly cut.

When I arrive home, there is a message from the nurse, left the afternoon before. Before I have a chance to return the call, two or three minutes later, my mother calls.

I just had to talk to someone she says. I don't know what's going on. I'm so angry and I'm so upset and I don't know why. I think I'm going crazy. She is crying. I think something's wrong with my brain and I don't know what's happening to me. I don't know what's going on. They brought my lunch to me here in my room and I don't know why they did that. I don't know what's happening. I haven't been out of my room all day and I haven't seen a soul and I'm just so worried I'm losing my mind.

I tell her that I understand what she's talking about. That it must be very hard to feel that way. That I love her.

She repeats herself. The lunch, the worries, the not knowing what's going on, the going crazy, the weeping.

I tell her that I understand what she's talking about. That it must be horrible to feel that way. That I love her.

I tell her to breathe.

I talk with her about what she can see out her window, about the kids, and slowly she calms down. By the time we get off the phone she is fairly calm. I call the nurse and learn that she insisted on having lunch in her room, that she is refusing to leave her room, that she has been crying off and on most of the last two days and that the medication doesn't seem to make much difference. The nurse explains that she is new, has only been there two weeks and just wanted to tell me all this because she isn't sure if this is out of the ordinary for my mother or not.

We drive through the snow, the large flakes swept up over the windshield, my wife beside me, my daughter in the back seat, watching the fields and yards and woods in the afternoon light diffused through the millions of snowflakes, covered in white. The car moves securely through the turns in the tree-lined drive. Shutting the car door makes only a soft, muffled thud, the snow absorbing all the sound.

Inside, there is an afternoon Valentine's Day tea, already begun, with residents seated on the living room chairs, the family members more often on folding metal chairs set up for the occasion, trays of tea and small cookies at various places around the room. I see my mother sitting at one end of one of the long couches, another woman at the other end and an empty place in the middle. Max takes a chair near one end of the sofa. I take a chair not far away. Renata sits next to her grandmother in the empty place on the couch, and the other woman looks at her and smiles. Renata smiles back.

At the other end of the room, in front of the French doors and the large windows, with the lake and the mountains behind her, a woman is playing a harp. The music is warm, clear, serene. I drink tea. I look at my mother, at my daughter, at the woman I don't know on the far side of my daughter. Each of them is rapt, looking at the woman playing the harp, their faces calm, their arms resting gently on their thighs, their fingers working away, delicately, keeping time.

Colorado, 1954

The first image runs lengthwise. In the background, the lower trunks of tall, thin trees. A man in the middle distance wears a fedora. He adjusts his cuffs. A harsh, stern woman leans in from the left like a sparrow hawk, her hand deformed by the motion and light of its forward thrust. A man with carefully slicked back hair, smoking a pipe, rests his left elbow on the picnic table. In the lower left hand corner, just above the border, nearly invisible against the white shirt of the man and the pale blouse of the sparrow hawk, my mother rests her chin on her hand.

Next comes a German shepherd, beside a thick tree. Sunlight in the distance falls on the grille of our Ford.

In the third, one whole side of the car is in a translucent bath of light. There are trees beyond: pines and other evergreens. In the foreground stands a man. His right foot rests on a rock, or perhaps the long seat of the picnic table or perhaps another car's bumper, his right forearm resting on his thigh, a man with thick, slightly curly hair, his sleeves rolled to the elbow, sun dappled across his chest, a small gun in a holster on his left hip, the handle facing forward.

Here a young boy stands in the shadows of the left foreground. I am just past him, looking at the camera, wearing my cowboy hat and dragging a large branch. I have a toy gun on my hip.

Next I stand about 15 feet away, at one end of a large tree that lies on the ground, my right hand on the handle of an axe sunk securely into the trunk.

Then I watch as my mother swings the axe, the blade a blur as she brings it down.

Later, one of the women leans over the table. Uncle Sig, my father's mother's brother, stands at the right.

Then the woman with the hawk face has a leg up on the plank seat, enters the frame of the picture from the left. She is alone here, in profile, pensive, handsome, her chin on her hand, looking into the distance.

My mother looks at the camera while my grandmother and the hawk-woman - who I think is my father's cousin, Emma - talk with Uncle Sig. Another woman pours from a thermos, serves to a boy and a girl.

These people move in and out of the remaining images. More children appear. At one point, I lean forward against a large tree, licking a water bag that hangs on the side of the tree while the other children stand nearby and, behind us, Uncle Sig watches, his arms folded, his hand at his mouth.

This outing in the summer sun, somewhere in the Rocky Mountains, up in the cool, filtered light of fir and aspen - lies along the earliest horizon of memory. I don't know who these people are now. Some are dead, others grown.

There is another, companion booklet, too.

My mother gives me something to drink, leans over me as I sit on the table, wiping my chin or inspecting something on my face or hand. My other hand rests on my gun. I wear suspenders.

Then the sparrow hawk leans forward, her head down. Sunlight angles through trees, and the other women all look at her.

Uncle Sig carves a walking stick.
One of the kids rides a burro.

Finally, I stand there, alone, looking this way, my arms at my sides. The afternoon shadows grow long.

The final image is from much later, after the car breaks down and we go back and then leave again. No people at all, just a stark shot of the car in front of a long, low motel with a faint tower for the power lines off in the distance, surrounded by the plains and sky.

Photograph: Small Leather Folder

I have the small leather folder in which my father carries pictures of my mother. It is in very good condition – two inches by three inches, light brown, machine stitched around the edges. On the cover, in the center, lies the Army Air Corps symbol – a propeller with wings – stamped in fake gold leaf.

The cover is lined with a dark pink satin, and the thumb slides across it easily as the folder is opened. On the right is a leather frame with stamped gold dots surrounding a picture of my mother taken by a professional portrait photographer, a head-and-shoulders shot in which my mother dissolves at the edges.

The photograph appears to have yellowed over the years, but in fact is in good condition, and it is the thick plastic designed to protect the photograph that has aged.

My mother is smiling, looking slightly above and to the right of the camera, her teeth showing in a small, dimpled smile, her cheeks smooth, her skin professionally aglow. On the back of the photograph, in my mother's handwriting, is her name and 1944, followed by a question mark in parentheses.

There is another photograph of her, too, loose, a snapshot that also has her name written on the back and the date 1940. The right-hand portion of the photo has been cut off so the photo will fit inside the folder. My mother stands with her arms stiffly at her sides, wearing a striped, belted dress with puffy shoulders, socks and shoes. She is smiling in this picture, too, but a different kind of smile. Behind her, about forty feet away, are a one-story brick bungalow, shrubs, a spindly tree, and a garbage can. The photograph is very worn, with hundreds of small creases arrayed around the central image of my mother, still whole.

The cover of the folder has a circular area in the middle that is darker than the surrounding leather - and, I discover, there is a matching area on the back. At first, I think the circle on the front is made by some object while the folder was in a pile in a box for all those years – a coin, perhaps. But when I discover the lighter, similar area on the back cover, I begin to think instead that these discolorations might be caused by something on his uniform, a button or badge on the pocket where he carries the folder, so that it depends on how he puts the folder in his pocket whether the button or badge presses into the front or back. I look through many photographs of him in uniform, attempting to confirm this, but cannot.

I look at these photographs of my mother once for every thousand times he looks at them. Then, much later, probably without giving it any thought, when he is back home and they are no longer needed, or no longer serve the same purpose, he stops.

It is sunny and hot. My son sits beside me while I drive. In the back sit my mother and my daughter. We are coming over the last hill on Harbor Road and my mother and daughter are giggling and playing a game with their hands on the space between them on the back seat. "This is my favorite part," says my mother, stopping the game suddenly. My daughter stops, too, quickly and easily, and cranes her head to see what my mother sees out the right side of the car, looking east. We are in the shadows of the trees to the west of the road, where the hill still ascends another 50 feet. To the east, in the sunlight, suddenly lies the bay, filled with sails, and beyond them, the mainland where we had been not very long ago. "And this means we're almost back," says my mother. My son looks quietly out the window, as if he were alone, able to create a kind of privacy with the character of his gaze, gathering gently and generously all that it can. At the hard curve at the bottom of the hill, my daughter asks if they can go back to playing now. My mother says yes.

I see my mother in her wheelchair at the round table. In front of her, a doll in a pink checkered dress. Her fingers move obsessively at the hem. The doll stares at the ceiling. I say hello.

My mother looks up at me and leans away. I say my name and she looks at me. One of the workers is there, watching us. My mother looks at her, then back at me, her head angled up, her hand still on the hem of the doll's dress.

I say my name. The woman who works there tells my mother that I am her son, that I have come to see her. My mother looks at me. I disengage the brakes on the wheels. I bring her to her room. She is very nervous.

I tell myself in no words that I already know about this, that I have read about it, have waited for it, have known it will be like this, but am still surprised, check myself, locate things in the room, make little plans to see me through the next five or ten seconds, fight the flood of what was never done or said and never will be while we continue to make something that is.

I sit in what used to be her chair and move her wheelchair close by. I say hello. She watches me. I smile. She says something, or tries to say something, or begins to say something, or wants to say something, or tries to say something, or is saying something somewhere deep inside her mouth, but her lips are too dry and stick to her teeth, so I lean closer, smell her sour breath, try to make words from the sounds and tiny expulsions of air, lean my ear next to her mouth, finally enter the tiny universe where the whispers and fragments and syllables collide and recombine, making new half-words in an old half-language, and she says, "There is a child."

I say yes, there is a child. She says no, another child. I say I am her son, that she is my mother, and I think of the other child, the child she lost at birth, the child that was only spoken of once, one summer evening, when I was 15, and I know that she isn't talking about that child, she is talking about another child, but if I tell myself that she is talking about that child, the lost one, then I will know what child she is talking about and in this way it will not be lost, and it will be up to me again to talk about another child, perhaps a child of mine, or to talk about being her child, so we can leave behind the other child she isn't talking about or not have to talk about the other child, and I say that the sun is shining, and look at the window, and she looks at the window, too.

After awhile she says something, and again I move my head very close to hers and she says "child" and "night" and "another" and "I" and "there was" and "night" and "a child." She looks at me with what looks like fear, but there is no fear, there is something else, but if I can use that word just for myself, even quietly, the way a word can be a word even when it is not spoken, then I can replace that with another word, without saying so, and maybe she won't be afraid, and I will have done something, even if there is no word for it, or nothing outside this room at all and just the sun comes in.

Smooth, round, fountain-pen

My father smiles broadly beneath a wide-brimmed fedora with a wide band, his left hand on the railing, the little finger of his left hand along the top of the railing and the other fingers hanging down, wearing a wide-lapel, double breasted suit, a high, tight collar and a tie. Behind him there is nothing, really. Only the faintest shapes or photographic artifacts. He is close to the camera, his body not visible below his right hand, which hangs at his side.

Morales Davis she writes - *newly discharged Air Force Sgt.* A date has been added - *3/1946.*

They are at a beach.

My mother is further away, and a little blurred. She leans back against the railing, her hands in the pockets of her fur coat, her feet crossed in front of her, looking tired, or anxious, or sad, or perhaps simply caught in the middle of a change of expression, an expression that perhaps is not at all indicative of her feelings. And she does look tired.

Beyond, beneath the top rung of the railing, there is a very narrow sliver of distant rocks or land or perhaps a wave.

On the back, much later, it seems, my mother writes Genevieve Davis. The smooth, round, fountain-pen writing of Morales Davis - newly discharged Air Force Sgt. is much older and earlier than the ballpoint Genevieve Davis, and the dating seems to have been done much later, too. On both prints, the date is written with the same ballpoint, and shows that both had originally been 3/1947 and then the 7's are changed to a 6's, the 7 now part of the lower loop of the 6, below a long stem. It is impossible to tell whether the time between when it reads 1947 and when it reads 1946 is measured in minutes or years, but it seems, from the more angular handwriting and the ballpoint pen it appears to be very long ago when she writes Morales Davis - newly discharged Air Force Sgt, and has a very different task now, such as organizing materials for a family album or scrapbook that is never made, an album that is to include many of the older photographs she has, some of them of people she doesn't know at all, and needs to record, as one often does on the back of such photos, when it is taken, and who these people are.

Essay on 9/11

Bill's essay contains many links which now, so long after the event, no longer work. Some, however, do. If you are reading this in a ebook, give them a try. Recognize, too, how responsible, and extraordinary, Bill's sense of responsibility as citizen journalist/historian was. How many of us without lost loved ones, simply went on with their lives, more sadly, perhaps, than before?
    (Editor's note from Marc Estrin)

1.

Around 9 in the morning, I take a break from finding news stories, reports and studies for the weekly online news service[1] I compile and edit for mental health professionals. As happens every now and then, the Internet has slowed to a crawl. While I wait for it to loosen up, I call the CEO of the business that funds the service, to chat, to catch up, to use the time well. I think he's in Pittsburgh, but he's driving through central Vermont, and asks right away if I know anything about a terrorist attack on the World Trade Center he just heard about on the radio. He says his brother works there. I turn the TV on, watch the smoke pour out of the floors near the top of the one tower and try to answer his questions about how it looks. I grew up in New York, worked in the financial district a long time ago. I ask which tower his brother works in, what floor. He says he's not sure which tower and thinks it's something like the 30th floor. I realize I just want to calm him, that I'm looking at the TV for reasons to say that his brother will probably be OK.

Right after we get off the phone, the second tower gets hit, and everyone who's watching sees it coming. I think about that a lot: we see it coming. My heart races with the horror of the reaction starting just before the act.

By a little after 10, the Pentagon has been hit, one of the towers has crumbled ("Oh my god," says the woman on the radio, "it's coming down. Oh my God...."), and I'm driving back up Route 7 to Burlington. The radio is on. I've been to the bank machine. I'm trying to decide whether to stay on Route 7 and go to the gas station, or take 189 over to Dorset Street to go get my 7-year old daughter from her school. My son is 14. It's his second week at the high school. He'll make good decisions on his own. He can catch the bus. My wife is downtown at a swimming class. She can catch the bus, too. But should I go get my daughter? Should I get my daughter and *then* get gas? Or should I get gas and just go home? I want to be home, but I want *everyone* to be home and none of them are. I think about the ice storm four years ago, the night we all slept in the living room while the trees came down around the house. I want us all in the living room again in our sleeping bags.

And at that exact instant of recollection, worlds collide, whole universes of experience that have always been entirely separate collapse and are suddenly fused by planes slamming into buildings hundreds of miles away, and I am making decisions about what turns to take based on what news announcers are telling me on my car radio. This has never happened before, and I want more information than I'm getting and none of it matters anyway.

I drive past the turnoff to 189. Then I hear reports of a plane down outside Pittsburgh, of buildings being evacuated across the country, of security precautions around Vermont's nuclear power plant, and think I may have made the wrong decision. Six miles – the distance between here and where my daughter is – suddenly seems like a great distance. I can imagine convoys and roadblocks, can remember huddling in the hallways of PS 161 in New York, can see the concentric circles on the maps printed in the newspapers. My breathing is different. I recognize my panic.

2.

A little after noon, I'm sitting in the living room with my wife. The TV has been on for an hour and a half, on within seconds of when I walk in the door. I watch the Pentagon burn beyond a stretch of highway, watch the smoke rise from the lower tip of Manhattan, watch the second plane fly into the second tower over and over, from several different angles, watch a cloud of ash and smoke roar up a downtown street, watch the same man, in shirtsleeves, emerge from the same cloud again and again.

After awhile, these images alternate with men in dark suits and crisp white shirts and red ties: outraged Congressmen on the roof of a building somewhere in Washington, think tank analysts, scholars, retired generals, ex-CIA men, fiction writers, former ambassadors, cabinet members from previous administrations, speech writers, spooks. In some ways, this is comforting. I have portioned out the time. "Let's see if anything else happens in the next 20 minutes." We slowly edge move to waiting until the end of the school day. The minutes accumulate since the last reported attack.

Finally, listening to Henry Kissinger blather on, I suddenly realize that the networks essentially stopped reporting news about 45 minutes earlier. Now there is simply this frightening spectacle, formulaic ways of presenting that spectacle, and an endless stream of ill-informed "experts." I still want information – I *desperately* want information – but the obligation to provide it has been replaced by the obligation to be somber, to provide an appearance of order, to not mention the silence and absence of the president, to fashion a kind of emotional glue of unfathomable loss, to remain business-like while the symbol of American business is a burning pile of twisted metal and concrete, to appear vigilant while the Pentagon burns. And I want information from *on the ground*, not from inside a TV studio.

I realize, too, that many questions have begun to accumulate. *What's happening in Europe and Asia? Are there attacks elsewhere? What made that plane come down in Pennsylvania? Are there a lot of people showing up at the emergency areas in New York? Are the markets still open in Europe? What are the reactions of the leaders of other countries? Was there really a bomb outside Congress? Are airports around the world shut down, too?* I watch the TV for another 15 minutes – watch ash-covered, weeping people who are very scared but know nothing, listen to TV announcers trying to describe what I can see behind them for myself, watch the second plane slam into the second tower a dozen more times, watch it fly into the second tower and poke out the other side, and, finally, I walk away. The worlds that had collapsed have already begun to spin away from each other again. I leave the world of television and go back to where I was when this all started three and a half hours ago - the Internet.

Online I found answers to almost all of my questions. There wasn't a bomb outside the Capitol. The markets in Europe are still open (the dollar dropping like a stone, oil futures were going through the roof, etc.). Warships are steaming out of the Mediterranean.

Other warships are gathering in the Indian Ocean. Airports around the world are also closed. There are riots in Indonesia. Israel is moving against Palestinian settlers. Russian troops are on the move. Explosions are reported in Afghanistan. I don't hear about any of this on American television for several hours. But online, I'm not restricted to what the networks think "the story" should be. There are many stories. I can go to the BBC, the Guardian, Al Ahram, the Palestinian Times, the Independent, the Hindustan Times, the Dominion Post, to Arab News, to the Electron Intifada, to Israel Insider, to the Gulf News, Reuters, The Times of India, to newspapers in any country in the world.

And I find much more than just news. As government agencies struggle to respond to the situation, Internet users themselves are responding. At the "Check-In Registry" site created by Bill Shunn[2], a programmer from Queens, people in NYC report that they're OK, or inquire about someone. By late that afternoon, though, the site is completely overwhelmed with traffic and others spring up, including the now-defunct *safe.millennium.berkeley.edu* site, whose opening page is dominated by two large, stark buttons. One says "I WANT TO LET PEOPLE KNOW I'M SAFE," the other, "I WANT TO FIND OUT IF SOMEONE IS SAFE." Soon come Sept11, the Hospital Patient Locator System[3], the private ny.com site that was confused with the City's official site, the Disaster Message Service[4] and a host of others.

Then there are the web logs, known to frequent users simply as "blogs." Blogs are personal and community sites that can be added to directly by users (see Blogger[5] for an example of the free software used to launch your own), and over the last year and a half a variety of Internet subcultures have grown up around blogs. Because I was working that morning, I didn't see right away just how quickly bloggers spread word of the attacks. At *Metafilter*, I find this post:

> Plane crashes in to the word trade center.[6] Apologies for not linking to anything besides the main CNN page but there are no full stories on this yet. The plane crashed into the building about six minutes ago, from what the TV is saying. We are about sixty blocks north and we can see the smoke over the skyline. posted by karen[7] at 5:58 AM PST - 491 comments[8].

Even at tech-oriented blogs like *Slashdot*[9], all conversation is about the attacks[10]. While the television networks move from news to analysis, people connected to the SlashDot community are asking and trying to answer questions themselves. Someone posts a message saying they'd spoken to a relative who works in the Capitol building, and that there was no explosion there. There are rumors of attacks at Camp David. Rumors that the plane down in Pennsylvania had been shot down. Someone reports lines at gas stations in Wisconsin and rapidly rising prices. Someone posts a link to a web version of the DC Special Operations Police Channel, filled with info on air

cover in the DC area: fighter, tankers, AWACS. There are scores of posts with links to pages of photos, some by professionals like Jeremy Kaiman[11], others by amateurs like Ziggy[12]. There's a post relaying news of explosions in Kabul, and that night, someone writes that "A group known as the Northern Alliance, an Afghan group opposed to the Taliban and associated with Shah Massooda, has taken credit for the explosions in Afghanistan." There are multiple posts confirming that a *second* propeller plane had been seen in the DC area following the one that crashed into the Pentagon. There is a lively discussion of whether you really can learn to fly a plane using *Microsoft Flight Simulator*. That night, too, come first hand reports from Wichita, Denver, Columbus, Cape Breton and Boston on military air traffic overhead. There are also countless messages of condolence, grief and sadness, only a handful of messages fueled by anger and hate. There was the full range of human reaction, emotion and experience - and this connection with people, I found, meant more to me than anything the TV announcers and politicians could ever say.

Millions of instant messaging and e-mail messages were sent on the 11th - messages inquiring about family and friends, messages detailing personal reactions. One study, by the Pew Charitable Foundation[13], indicates that general use of the Internet was actually down in the days following the attack, as casual users stayed away entirely and its use for shopping and entertainment plummeted. But people (like me) who use the net heavily used it *more* than usual – there was a huge spike in traffic at US news sites - and beyond providing information, the Internet also provided channels of expression and action. Over four million people turned to the Internet because the phones weren't working well enough for them – and Internet users were more likely than non-users to try to contact loved ones and friends during those days.

Pew reports, too, that "Internet users were more likely than nonusers to display some kinds of emotional and civic engagement with their country: online Americans were among the most fervent to attend meetings and attempt to donate blood." The afternoon of the attacks, a nationwide network of quilters had already posted plans for a WTC Memorial Quilt.[14] By that evening, a Danish site offered the opportunity to light a virtual candle[15]. At Beliefnet.com[16], 2400 online "prayer circles" were started – and a special section on Islam was heavily visited.

III.

Within days, the volunteer registries of survivors and victims had all been overwhelmed by data, by traffic and by problems - and official sites were up and running. The slapdash, handmade pages of photos and first-hand accounts began to be replaced by sites that reflected more time and effort, more design values. News organizations moved away from images of the crashes to sophisticated graphics detailing the attack on the WTC[17] and the Pentagon[18], the path of the plane[19] that crashed in Pennsylvania, animations of the WTC towers collapsing[20], profiles of "Bin Laden and his group[21]," maps of hospitals, staging areas and blood donation centers in New York[22], graphics detailing how people in the WTC managed to "escape from high rise hell[23]" and how rescue workers were shoring up the Pentagon[24]. And there were images and graphics and animations everywhere - a gallery of newspaper front pages from around the world[25], a map showing the countries of origin of the victims[26].

At the time, I found many of those graphics disturbing, though not in the same way as the endless replays of the plane hitting the tower. Eventually, a kind of familiarity or numbness took over as the videos were repeated. Even the clips ignored by the networks but widely available online of people jumping and falling somehow confirmed that the spectacle of the plane and the flames helped obscure the essential truth here - *there were people in there who died horrible deaths*. By contrast, there was something slick, antiseptic, and immediately distancing about all these fancy newspaper graphics. The very sophistication of something like MSNBC's "The Darkest Day[27]" felt stilted, manipulative, and false. I preferred the reality of Jim Galvin's stunning panoramic images of Ground Zero[28], which I explored for more than an hour.

Within weeks, of course, the images of that day had been largely left behind. A few images – firemen raising a flag –became cultural icons, but the photos and interactive graphics had a new subject – the war in Afghanistan. The *BBC* provided clickable maps[29], the *Times* a graphical history lesson on the country[30], the *Washington Post* a "War Zone Explorer.[31]"

But even as the focus moved from the site of the attacks to Afghanistan, from the destruction here to the war there, and from detailed reports to "interactive" graphics, writing continued to appear that captured events and experiences that seemed to be getting lost in the media shuffle, events and experiences that seemed to me for some reason very important to retain. I wept when I read Steven Jay Gould's "Ground Zero's vital crumbs of comfort[32]," was left in awe by Chris Smith's portrait of the firefighters of Squad 18, "Braving the Heat[33]." Like many others, I read the New York Times' thumbnail profiles of victims, "Portraits of Grief[34]," every day.

By late September and early October, a glut of new personal web sites and new blogs focused entirely on the attacks and their aftermath. Many, like *Life During Wartime*[35] and *WTC-Filter*[36], are already the Internet equivalent of archaeological artifacts. Others, like Attack in America, are simply gone. Some, like *World New York*[37], have moved on or returned to other themes and subjects. And the accounts of witnesses and survivors were also succeeded by very different kinds of online ventures - "war blogs," composed of personal commentary with embedded links to news stories, articles and essays. Among the most prominent are those by Jeff Jarvis[38], Matt Welch[39], Ken Layne[40] and Andrew Sullivan[41]. In early October, as an outgrowth of obsessive e-mails to a handful of friends, I started a blog of my own, Victory Coffee[42], though it includes no commentary, just links to articles, news stories, essays, photos and Internet oddities.

By early 2002, most of the war blogs (including my own) were losing steam. The BBC did a magnificent series in early December, "NYC: Out of the Ashes[43]," and since then coverage of New York slid to less visible and prominent pages. *City Pages* had a very moving "Postcard from Ground Zero[44]" around the same time. The Sunday before New Year's Day, the *Times* published the final installment of Portraits of Grief[45] and discontinued its special A Nation Challenged section. The CNN site still heralds the "War Against Terror[46]," but at the *Washington Post* site today, the lead story was about the hiring of a football coach. Even the site devoted to following up the many rumors that arose on September 11 and 12 is now titled *Rumors of War*[47].

By now, too, of course, the fires are finally out. And as the attacks of September 11 (and the war they spawned) are absorbed back into the ongoing flow of events around the world, their impact is much less visible, the voices that speak of them less personal.
Firefighters have weighed legal actions[48] against the city of New York. Families of victims have formal advocacy organizations (with very professional web sites), like Families of September 11[49] and the WTC United Family Group[50]. Even at the Red Cross site[51], the first screen of info has the solitary, almost sad link, "Help is still available for the victims of September 11[52]." One WTC Memorial site[53] has been ignored for more than a month, but there are many, many others – the *National Fallen Firefighters Foundation*[54], the *World Away* site, the *American Memorials* site[55]... the list goes on and on[56].

The Library of Congress and the Pew Charitable Trust[57] have begun the *September 11 Archive*, a collection of archived documents commissioned by the Library of Congress "to preserve digital materials covering the events of September 11, 2001." The collection presently contains 5 terabytes of data, and the full index of archived sites[58] would take years to browse. Sometimes I just hit a few links to see what's there. Tonight, I turned up "The Stars Seem Farther Away Without the Stairway," a September 14 piece by NYU's John Laxmi published, off all places, in *The Hindu*, a page with a link to an audio file of Louis Farrakhan's press conference on the attacks at *The Final Call* (didn't listen, though), an *Alternative Asian Voices* page with info on missing Bengladeshis, and a handmade memorial page that has a button link to another handmade page with the simple text "I remember. Do you?"

I do remember, want never to forget, and realize this will take some effort. I'm thankful for the September 11 Archive[59], for the personal bookmarks files I've kept, for the sites that still preserve some sense of what those awful days were like when I felt so utterly human, so aware of what was and was not important, when the human cost of politics was so clear, when the skies were silent and empty. I still go back to sites like *Missing Pieces*[60], for example, and reread Leslie Harpold's piece about making sandwiches for rescue workers, and Edward Kink's story of escaping from the 23rd floor of Tower 2. There is something in these stories I do not want to lose sight of, something the Internet allowed me to connect with, even from here in Vermont, on dark, quiet September nights. I especially like the ending of the piece "Recording[61]," written September 13th by Grant Barrett, a Columbia student and creator of the elegant, very literate blog *World New York*[62], which roams the web nearly every day and "attempts to direct your attention to some of the good bits before they vanish". His writing there is worldly, literate, erudite. By contrast, "Recording[63]" is simple, personal, anecdotal, and concludes:

My heart is in this now, but my efforts are feeble. I am allergic to the chemical smoke, which when the wind blows seaward, I can taste on the bitter edges of my tongue even at home in Brooklyn. I cannot contribute financially to the relief. I have no belongings to give, except perhaps socks. So I sit at my computer for hours, reading personal stories, linking, writing, promoting, weaving a thin network of human beings and their stories. It's a small thing, but it is a record.

2001-2002

Endnotes/Links
1. http://www.cccinternational.com/pulse/latestpulse.htm
2. http://news.cnet.com/news/0-1014-201-7147460-0.html
3. http://147.208.4.54/wtc/search.asp
4. http://66.40.240.240/dmstest/america.html
5. http://www.blogger.com/
6. http://www.cnn.com/
7. http://www.metafilter.com/user.mefi/1668
8. http://www.metafilter.com/mefi/10034
9. http://slashdot.org/
10. http://slashdot.org/article.pl?sid=01/09/12/0251205&mode=thread
11. http://www.jkaiman.com/wtc_map.html
12. http://ziggy.dreamland.net/wtc/
13. http://www.pewinternet.org/
14. http://www.wtcmemorialquilt.com/
15. file:///Users/billdavis/Desktop/lightacandle.sol.dk
16. http://www.beliefnet.com/
17. http://a188.g.akamaitech.net/f/188/920/15m/www.washingtonpost.com/wp-srv/nation/graphics/attack_ny091101.htm
18. http://a1022.g.akamai.net/f/1022/6000/5m/www.latimes.com/media/graphic/2001-09/643975.gif
19. http://www.nytimes.com/library/national/index_TRACKER02.html
20. http://www.usatoday.com/graphics/news/gra/wtccollapse/frame.htm
21. http://www.washingtonpost.com/wp-srv/nation/graphics/binladen_091301.htm
22. http://www.nytimes.com/library/national/index_SEARCH.html
23. http://www.smh.com.au/news/0109/14/graphics/14wldescape.gif
24. http://www.washingtonpost.com/wp-srv/nation/graphics/attack/pentagon_4.html
25. http://www.interactivepublishing.net/september/
26. http://www.thetimes.co.uk/article/0%2C%2C3-2001322462%2C00.html
27. http://www.msnbc.com/news/attack_front.asp?launch=/modules/wtc_terror_experience/default.asp
28. http://www.pixpi.com/groundzero/qtindex.html
29. http://news.bbc.co.uk/hi/english/static/in_depth/world/2001/war_on_terror/key_maps/
30. http://www.nytimes.com/library/national/index_EMPIRE.html

31. http://www.washingtonpost.com/wp-srv/flash/photo/map_explorer/frames_region.htm
32. http://www.guardian.co.uk/international/story/0%2C3604%2C558667%2C00.html
33. http://www.newyorkmetro.com/news/articles/wtc/smith1.htm
34. http://www.nytimes.com/pages/national/portraits/index.html
35. http://www.killyourtv.com/wartime/
36. http://wtc.blogspot.com/
37. http://www.worldnewyork.org/
38. http://crisis.blogspot.com/
39. http://mattwelch.com/warblog.html
40. http://www.kenlayne.com/
41. http://www.andrewsullivan.com/
42. http://www.howardstreet.com/news
43. http://news.bbc.co.uk/hi/english/in_depth/americas/2001/nyc_out_of_the_ashes/newsid_1695000/1695373.stm
44. http://citypages.com/databank/22/1096/article9998.asp
45. http://www.nytimes.com/pages/national/portraits/index.html
46. http://www.cnn.com/
47. http://www.snopes2.com/rumors/rumors.htm
48. http://www.newsmax.com/showinside.shtml?a=2001/12/1/95704
49. http://www.familiesofseptember11.org/home.asp
50. http://www.wtcunitedfamilygroup.org/
51. http://www.redcross.org/
52. http://www.redcross.org/news/ds/0109wtc/donationwork/stillhere.html
53. http://www.thewtcmemorial.com/
54. http://65.89.45.6/
55. http://www.americanmemorials.com/NationalTragedy.htm
56. http://www.researchbuzz.com/911/memorials.html
57. http://september11.archive.org/
58. http://web.archive.org/collections/sep11/full_list.html
59. http://september11.archive.org/
60. http://fray.com/hope/pieces/leslie.html
61. http://fray.com/hope/pieces/grant.html
62. http://www.worldnewyork.org/
63. http://fray.com/hope/pieces/grant.html

made again a firmament

"Lapis lazuli, or lapis for short, is a deep blue metamorphic rock used as a semi-precious stone that has been prized since antiquity for its intense color...."

the name I couldn't remember
is *lapis lazuli*
not the small round uniform crystals
of industrial ultramarine
mass-produced since 1828
but large irregular prisms
secluded in molecular chambers of stone
each allowing different amounts
of light to pass through
a *blue beyond the sea*
embedded with calcite mica and quartz
the speckles of pyrite creating an impression
not of stars but of a firmament
from which stars fell thousands of years ago
were shattered across the high slopes
of the Kokcha Valley
where huge fires were built
then splashed with water
splitting the rock into pieces
that could be carried away
smeared across the walls of caves
taken to Cairo as *the sky stone*
spilled across the breastplates of royalty
fashioned into pendants and bracelets and rings
shaped into the eye of Isis
watching as souls pass and depart
shaped into a heart
and etched with the 26th chapter
of *The Book of the Dead*

endlessly ground to powder
treated with tinctures and pastes
added and stirred
slowly above a flame
by apprentices and apothecaries
plunged into buckets of ice
kneaded and cooled
and rubbed and mixed
with two ounces of pearl-ashes,
dissolved in a pint of water, then filtered
used as a remedy for melancholy and fever
used to make water and sky
made again a firmament by Raphael
secluded by Vermeer in the serenity
 of *Woman Holding A Balance*
and even in the shaded white draperies
black marble tiles, green foliage and
whitewashed walls of *The Glass of Wine*
imparting knowledge it is said
old enough to reconnect the heart and mind
pried loose with picks and shovels
by prisoners chained to the walls of the shafts
carried by horses and ships and wagons
made into columns for a cathedral in St. Petersburg
(a pound of silver for a pound of stone)
mined in the 1980's using ordinance
from land mines left behind by the Russians
smuggled out of Kabul three years ago
and trucked through the dust and snow to Peshawar
rising and dropping and rising in price

but always shimmering
not really crystals at all
but a zone of subatomic lenses and veins
tender flaws that only reveal
their full translucence
over weeks or months
and do not fade in the light

Still Life Press
2005

I wanted/to tell /to ask

1

Nine of Wands

I wanted to tell you about the wind one night last week.

I wanted to tell you how loud it was, how it sounded like there were sirens outside.

I wanted to tell you that when I opened the porch door, the wind pushed back, and tried to hold it shut, and that when I forced the door open and went out, there were sirens, and how a few minutes later the wind and the sirens both stopped.

I wanted to tell you that later that night, just as I was going to bed, it came up all at once from everywhere again, like a massive current desperate to complete some circuit through the little cities and roads out to the mountains, and how it was so loud once, I was afraid.

I wanted to tell you I heard each resonance in the spaces between the buildings shred and multiply, heard the sculpting, emptying, scouring sound of some disembodied, banished god come screaming in off the lake to the towers of landing lights just up the river from here, past the turbines and abandoned mills.

I wanted to tell you it sounded like something running for its life, how the windows chattered like teeth and the trees couldn't stop shaking, and I knew I was just made of bones - of bones and things that can be stripped from bones - and how whatever I was afraid of then passed, soared off in less than a heartbeat, and ask if you've ever felt that way, too.

I wanted to tell you I stood there, just this side of the door, waiting for it to retreat. How I sat for a minute on the edge of a bed, turned on a reading lamp, adjusted a few things and put them away.

I wanted to ask you if you were awake then, too, if you remember the night I'm talking about and heard that wind. I wanted to tell you I couldn't sleep at all until late, when it was quiet again, the way it is now, the way it is tonight.

2

Six of Cups

I wanted to ask what forgiveness is for you and how it works. Not what you say to someone, but what you say to yourself that lets you say whatever you say later to them, and if you need to always say something, and if you think we can keep forgiveness to ourselves without forgetting some of what we need to remember. Sometimes I think forgiveness involves some special skill we need to learn as we get older, and sometimes it just seems like one of those ideals we're supposed to live up to, like love, that no one really does too well with, some abstract shorthand for something that, most of the time, looks just as messy as everything else, and wonder if that's why sometimes it seems there's more to forgive than we'll ever have time for, and other times it seems like it would be so easy, if we could just forget all the particulars.

I wanted to ask, when you think about forgiving someone, how you know that you have. Sometimes, I'll think I've forgiven someone for something they've said or done, but later, I'll remember what happened and get upset about it all over again. I wanted to ask if this ever happens to you, and whether you think that means you haven't really forgiven them, or if there are always things left over that upset us, and if they're part of what we need to remember.

I wanted to ask you how you can tell what you need to forgive and what you don't when there's so much you might need to, some of it just a lot of little, insignificant things, too small to even bother with by themselves, that sometimes can accumulate and turn into something else, turn into more than you know what to do with, and ask you if there's some threshold or critical mass involved for forgiveness to be necessary, and how we know when we reach it, and ask whether you think it makes any difference to ask to be forgiven, or to be asked, and why it seems so much harder to forgive someone who doesn't say they're sorry, or doesn't forgive us, when that doesn't really change what we need to forgive them for in the first place, or if it does, and if them saying they're sorry or not saying they're sorry (or saying they forgive us or not saying they forgive us) are part of what we need to remember or part of what it's OK to forget, and what we can do when we make mistakes and end up getting things backwards, when we forget and then forgive, and whether anything is ever the same afterwards.

I wanted to ask you about the not forgetting, because I don't always know what to do with what we're supposed to not forget, except that it shouldn't become like a grudge that weighs us down, and ask if you think you should always keep those kinds of things to yourself, or whether there are times when you should say what they are, and what you can do to protect the forgiveness then, or if you think it all depends on how big a deal something is, and if it's alright to talk about things the charge or force have already gone out of, either slowly, the way memories get pushed aside by other memories, or suddenly, the way a light bulb will just die, or if sometimes we're better off quietly dragging around our own ragged sacks of ruined things, trying to forgive ourselves or forget ourselves, and just leave each other in peace.

I wanted to ask if you remember how the sunlight looked on the river when we came up the stairs, how we walked a little ways and then crossed that bridge, twice, and how, on our way back, four older men were setting up to play music as a crowd gathered, and how happy everyone seemed, and how there didn't seem to be anything that needed to be forgiven, at least that afternoon, not just in our lives, but in the lives of all the people around us, people we had never seen before who happened to be crossing that same bridge, and how the sun was so strong that day and the river was flled with so many boats.

3

Ten of Swords

I wanted to ask you tonight about being lost. Not about driving back and forth across the toll roads of that sunlit strip, not about coming through the fairy houses in the woods to that fork in the path the little map didn't show, but about what we mean when we say we feel lost, or that something about our lives seems lost, wanted to ask you how something about your life can be lost if you still know what it is, ask you why sometimes remembering is enough and sometimes it just makes everything worse.

I wanted to tell you I'm not so sure. I wanted to tell you I wore these shoes in the sun up the cobblestones in the graveyard, through the gate in the fence in that hilltop meadow and up the dirt road from the only dock, and that something about those places remains, something about me corresponds to them, even if something about who I was when I walked there is gone, and tell you sometimes I just want all those places to disappear, and other times I can't stop them from disappearing.

I wanted to ask what you do when you know something in you is there but you just can't find it when you need to. I wanted to ask why things about you that you've lost can still pull at you so, ask what could possibly fill this next minute or this next week, ask what you use for reins.

I wanted to ask you why what's lost can seem to matter so much, and if this means that some things won't ever be lost, or if it just reminds us that everything gets lost, sooner or later, and if this is something we should try to get more accustomed to as we get older or should try to resist.

I wanted to tell you the fairy houses looked like beautiful, ruined dreams of some other world, a child's dream or an old dream as deep as the world is, something not given but made, and that they looked like they were abandoned as soon as they were built, the forlorn walls of twigs stuck in the loam, the little flap of moss for an awning, the wreckage of something still incompletely imagined, places where only dreams could have ever lived but never occupied, places lost the moment they were found. Sometimes I think when we say we feel lost we don't mean something about our lives, really, but about the stories we tell ourselves about our lives, and I wanted to ask what you do when things happen that don't ft into the stories, and if you've ever tried to make something ft that didn't, and what happened to you when you did that, or if you change the story so that what happened *does* fit, and ask what you do then with all the things that need to be changed, especially if they're from a long time ago or are important things, and whether you go back through all the different trajectories, adjusting things, discarding some like clothes you know you won't wear again, or whether things just disappear from the stories on their own.

I wanted to tell you that sometimes it feels like something about who I am isn't there anymore, or is contracting, or just isn't needed and has nothing left to do, and I wanted to tell you I feel this way sometimes not because anything about my life has changed, but because everything around it has, like when you're driving back at night from a trip, tired, lost in images of statues and lawns and gardens and the faint music, and something happens that's like waking up, and you realize you have no recollection at all of the last ten miles, and your breath catches and you tighten your grip on the wheel.

I wanted to tell you that for me the stories can all be forgotten or dismantled or overwhelmed, and images will still remain, drifting off from the loose gravitational pull of the narratives, some essentials the stories can't be reduced to, things freed from all the unnecessary complications - a blanket of darkened sky, a clot of trees, the soft rain's embrace - keeping what the stories can't hold anymore wrapped safely in their folds and branches and arms, even as what connects you to the story of the events that spawned them keep slackening their ropes.

I wanted to tell you that something like the shape of a chain of leaves floating on the surface of a river still pulls whole geographies through my legs and chest, no matter how much has been lost.

I wanted to talk to you not about losing yourself in something, not about leaving things about your life behind and losing yourself for a few days on an island or losing yourself for a long time in something about your life that extends beyond you, but what happens when you stop being able to lose yourself that way, what happens when the ferry returns or you come back to what you thought you'd left, when something about your life is suddenly gone and where once you could lose everything about yourself there, now you just lose the pieces that were broken off, that fell away or came loose, the things life has gone out of, the facts that don't ft anymore in the world.

I wanted to tell you that my book is exactly where I put it on the table, that my shoes are still there by the door where I took them off, that my coat is still draped over the same arm of the same chair, but something here is like a face I've come to know so well I can make its shape in the dark with my fngertips, and that something about who I am has hands, too, and keeps making that shape everywhere in the empty air and the lamplight, and ask if that's ever happened to you.

I wanted to ask if your life is more like a book or a painting, like a sheaf of pages that grows larger as you get older, with pages that get shuffed and rearranged and maybe scattered around in different piles or places, or if earlier versions are gradually covered as new layers are smeared across the surface, even if the brighter colors are all translucent and some vestige of a bench at the end of a dock, or a simple mortar and pestle on a countertop will still show for awhile through their veils, and if the process then is simply repeated until the surface is entirely new, the foor of vision brought that much closer, so that winding your way ceremonially through a circle of sun-bleached buoys stuck in the sand like idols doesn't show at all in the new arrangement, but still resides there somewhere, hidden in the accumulated topography, and ask if you think it's true that for a painter *time is measured by the stimulus of grinding and mingling tiny prisms* - or, if your life is more like a handful of pages, what does the work of the prisms, and what you use to grind them.

I wanted to tell you that to be lost is to be defeated, to be wasted, to spend things in vain, and is derived from an archaic word whose past participle, *loren*, only survives now in parts of other words, like *forlorn* or *lovelorn*, and that *to lose* means, really, to perish, and in the hypothetical reconstructed ancestral language of the Indo-European family *to lose* is *to cut off*, to untie, to separate, its roots in Sanskrit also in the words for *cuts* or *cuts off* and the word for *sickle*, in the Greek for loosen, untie, slacken, in the Latin for *release* or *atone for*, and ask what you use to cut off the things about yourself you feel falling away, or what in you loosens something so that other parts of you can be untied, and if you think anything atones for what's been lost, tell you that the phrase *at a loss* didn't come along until the late 16th century has to do with hounds losing a scent, or that *forget* means, literally, to lose one's grip, and that the word *fairy* has something to do with the word *fate*, and that *house* is connected to the old verb *to hide*, or that in some of the stories fairies lure humans out to their islands, where everything is happiness and no one gets old or gets sick, but there's no escape, and that by now all of these things are hidden, and have been for a long time, lost in the woods, lost in the words.

I wanted to tell you about the low band of clouds moving across the sky tonight, just above the rooftops, and how the clouds would slide out from behind the hill to the west like a wide ribbon on a giant spool, though there didn't seem to be any wind down here at all, and how that band of clouds kept moving and changing, passing the way a strip of flm moves through an antique magic lantern, the crank and flywheel secluded by the hills or behind the buildings, and ask you what the blade is that slips between the images and makes them appear to move as they pass and disappear into the trees above the streetlights.

4

Five of Cups

I wanted to ask you tonight how you think about your soul, not all the things in that other, unfinished letter. Sometimes I think my soul is just something my brain makes up. Or a story I tell myself. And I know sometimes what I mean when I say "my soul" and what I mean when I say "my heart" can get mixed up, along with a lot of other things.

I wanted to ask when you first noticed your soul.

I wanted to ask that when I was four or five, I'd heard the word "soul" at church, but didn't have any idea, really, about having one, and that by the time I was 14 or 15, I did, sort of, so for me it was somewhere in-between.

I wanted to ask you whether you think the soul is something that starts small and grows like we do, until we notice it, or if it's something we just find over time, as we learn how to.

I wanted to tell you about picking up Alan Watts at the Erie International Airport in the spring of 1971, and how the other person in the car, a young woman who I didn't really know, asked what he thought of astrology, and he said that the basic idea was a good one - the body inside the soul, not vice versa, and all the heavens a map of the soul - but the problem is the maps are thousands years out of date, and wanted to tell you the map of my soul already feels out of date, wouldn't need as much sky as I see through this window and ask if you ever feel that way, too, tell you sometimes I really don't know what's inside what.

I wanted to ask if you think our souls are something about us that our bodies hide, or something that isn't attached to us at all, or aren't even ours.

I wanted to ask, when you look at a chair someone has been sitting in, if the chair is empty now, if you ever think you see traces where their soul passed, or if that's just a kind of thing people say to themselves at those times when they think they know better.

I wanted to tell you there was something about how old the walls were, about the fields of poppies not yet blooming, about all that sky, about what that old couple was trying to say, and about why it was so important to them to say it that afternoon, about the green through the window slits in the towers, that changed something about my soul and I don't even know all of what beyond the images I still carry of that day, and wanted to ask you if you think there are times when our souls can shift, or settle, or turn.

I wanted to ask you if you think the soul can get sick, and if it can, if it's contagious, ask you what you think makes it better, and whether it can get different sicknesses, whether there are different treatments for those different sicknesses, and whether you think it can be healed or not, if there's anything we can do to keep our soul from getting sick, and what happens if you don't know what to do when it does.

I wanted to ask you if you think our souls can really be damaged and broken, like a thing, or wounded and injured, like something that lives and dies, or whether you think the soul is something that can't be damaged or broken or wounded or injured, even if it feels that way sometimes, and if whatever feels that way then is something different.

I wanted to ask if what you know about your soul is something that makes you feel better. Sometimes it is for me, but sometimes it isn't, and I don't know what to do then, because it's supposed to, or at least it's supposed to help you notice more or see things differently, and a lot of the time I don't know what I'm doing wrong or maybe just missing.

I wanted to ask if you've ever dreamed about your soul and what your soul is like in your dreams and if it's different. Sometimes I dream that someone dead is alive, and when I wake up, I don't remember they're dead, because I'd just been talking to them, and it takes me a minute or two to realize they're gone, but I think that has more to do with my soul than theirs.

I wanted to ask you if you think that something about the soul stays everywhere you go, if it stretches and gets larger as you get older and go more places, or if you think we leave some part of it wherever we go, and if those parts are ever connected, somehow, or ever gathered somehow, or if you think we just bring things back with us from different places in our souls, whether there are places we haven't been to that our souls need us to go, what we won't know if we don't go, what those places are for you, which ones you've been to already, and whether you think they're different places for everybody, and what happens when some of the places are the same.

I wanted to ask if you think your soul has changed since we last talked, or if you think it ever changes. Sometimes, I think my soul does. Other times, I think what changes is everything else, and my soul stays pretty much the same. Maybe I only notice the changes after they've happened, and it seems like it's always been that way.

I wanted to tell you that most of the time my soul is like a picture that hangs on the kitchen wall - a picture, say, of a small chair in which there is a small statue and a small container overflowing with flowers - a picture I don't even notice most days, but notice sometimes, and know I would constantly feel the empty space there if I took the picture down, even if looking at it today is hard because of everything it reminds me of.

Still Life Press
2005

The Coach Road Landscapes

Meadow Bordered by Trees,
Pierre-Étienne-Théodore Rousseau, 1845

The torrent was wild, the storms were wonderful, but the most wonderful thing of all was how we ourselves, the dream and I, ever got here. By our feet we could not - by the clouds we could not - by any ivory gates we could not – in no other way could we have come than by the coach road.

        John Ruskin
        The Works of John Ruskin: Volume 6

The way the streets smelled in the middle of April reminded me of something about hope I once knew. So do the things gathered here. They may be filled with land and light and water, but all take paintings, photographs and prints as their points of departure - images of places we may not have seen, but still can recognize by what moves through them, toward and away from us, and find what they render also rendered in fields and rivers and lives. The sources are all given at the end, though in each of the poems they're at some point left behind. My language for all this may be very different than theirs (or yours), and you may have other images or know different places along the way without it being a different road.

When a hillside I see is changed by hills I have only seen painted, when photographs float on impossible reservoirs of memory of a time long before I was born, when I look at the sky and try to discard all the images I've seen of other skies, when I take off my shoes and socks to work barefoot in the soil with a battered pitchfork, one of the blades half gone, another bent, I have the feeling of some circuit trying to be completed, some residual charge within things or in the spaces between things - spaces that ring, spaces that weep, spaces with weight and fragrance.

There may be no other way we could have come, but there's nothing final here. New things will appear and some have already been lost. Where they lead keeps changing, too. That's what always happens. That's what there's hope for.

Where I would wash
my rags and bones
triangular leaves
make footsteps in the air
on strings above bare dirt.

Where I would listen
peeling sounds
distract the animals
fixed to the roof and walls.

Where I would look for a door
there is a door
a want of adhesion
where things can wait.

I don't know if those are clouds
or a pure field of light
where things appear to start
or to disperse.

What resembles a line of breakers
crosses and moves away
but even that isn't clear.

That's what makes everything
dictated by age or illness
so harsh and so beautiful.

Some recurring angle perhaps
originating from a chair
comes to be repeated
more at the edges now than at sea.

Opening
of an unnamed place
to a wide path
air swollen
green with grasses.

Opening in light
the river only intensifies.

Opening protected
by splendid boughs
half-heard wings extend.

Opening of the heart
the head turns.

Opening you come to
undisturbed
little secrets left in memories
branches dipped in the river.

for Bud

Everything the sea drives off
sunlight still lifts
from leaves and branches.

The deformed trunk
of no real concern.

What's lacking isn't personality
but the urge to even include it.

Even the horizon isn't sure
where it's supposed to be.

The ground answers
by rising
slightly parallel
and somehow related to the tree
an exercise in patterns
overcoming a sense of place.

The women gather
what they can.
One kneels.
One reaches into a tree.

The only things
moving out there
are dying reflections
the surface can't hold
much longer.

Here is a coat
or blanket or tarp
there the unreal softness of trees.

Coming this way
inconspicuous flowers of sedge
down to a chimney the shape of a flame
time approaches
a low juncture of shining fields
cradles a gathering of rooftops
weary and bright with masks
the way the heart can look
for somewhere to rest
without rest.

The sky looks so big
I could fall almost anywhere
and still fall to this road.

The necessarily long exposures
lead to these shadowy forms.

Extensively retouched
the world looks ravished
almost posed.

What can he be doing in there?

Only one arm
is visible in the light
only the slightest
suggestion of a head or face
hedges and flowers
the height of his thighs.

How the endings keep changing
the way sound falls
further up the hill
beyond images we carry
of wrapped implements
 and brooms of twigs.

There are so many blossoms
coming in from the river
where she rises from a meadow
paths barely suggested
in grasses filling with light.

If you could relive
just one day of your life
this would be one of the ones
you would forsake
for being too perfect
yet always want
on the day you do choose
never to forget
to imagine complete.

One carries a ladder
someone not seen
must hold the other end
the inaudible progress
of wooden wheels
on a worn road
above a row of arches
greens in the weeds
the water inverts.

Where a bridge leads
an untouched village appears
to preserve the old ways
in thousands of small gestures
 broad faces of walls
half in shadow
half washed with light
the sky flickers above.

There is almost no subject
but those two by the riverbank
one walking as the other rides
 receding in opposite directions
as patterns of light and shadow
converge above the earth
where they must have passed
all the things not said or done
things withheld in brightness
the lessons all learned too late
stakes driven long ago into the earth
they find they would return to
or maybe they arrive too soon
promises still accumulating
beyond what can be seen
and only glimpse in passing
air the color of evaporated rust
the way one looks back
and the other doesn't
houses past the river
lit between the trees.

Boot prints in the wet ground
make little oceans
fill with silence
all the colors of the moon.

It's been another long day
and now that it's over
there's darkness everywhere
threads pulled loose
the silence listens for.

Between the living
and the not living
a mangled sun still shows
waves of broken colors.

Nothing separates
the sea and sky
storm petrels in flight
from what approaches
the smell of souls
flooding with power and danger
eyeless faces
scattered in the water
not yet obscured
by swells and spouts
history would erase.

Some undreamed place where
the world appears bright and
whole as a fisheye
to tilt and heave and slide away
as useless arms
almost triumphant
reach for soiled light
from chains that float.

Walls and windows flatten
when the dark trees lift
the crowded hills
cling to the smell of thunder
and the way disappears
not guided by memory
as it bends and fails.

So much had to be left out
curtains vaporized
where it all comes
to repeat itself
wave after wave.

All the light
won't stop bleeding
learns to breathe water
air the taste of hot chalk
covers us in salt.

How one loves
the frail protective tissue
embroidered of bowers
blotting out the world
a bright mosaic of scraps
of stars shredded and
collapsed after veering
too close
to some conduit or source
now streaming again
untranslatable
fountains of auroras
specks of pendants the size of tears
obscuring how it is still possible
roses would spill.

You have to wonder where
those two are from
if she even sees what she is
so abstracted from
if he senses the stares
of the others now averted
or even cares for fishing
with only the idea of a line
not breaking the surface
everywhere you look
already broken.

A deliberate tree at the center
an array of stranded bodies thousands of raw
parcels of spring each the length and
width of a finger pointing in every
direction
in hot sheaves from hidden ground.

The shiver of it all
as intentional as in a dream
the man exhausted
before he collapsed.

Not the one fishing
not the one drinking the sky
not the one with a hat in a little boat
but the one who sprawls on his side
in his sleep dreams faces of paste
legs wrapped like wafers
littered on a teeming hillside
a sky patched with weeds
a boat that knows nothing of pain.

These few buildings stand
void of all sentiment
against the ocean's onslaught.

All those shapes
the water makes
must have been remembered.

Yes, these people live hard lives.

Waves fall
on their representations.

If I could go back
 nothing would change
the heat removed
from the ashes of the sky
insignificant details
that tell the whole story
you can't begin to imagine
standing in the emptiness
open veins of gravity
drained and colorless
where we would return
to be fixed
on some reconstructed horizon
negatives joined
as if nothing had happened
where the sky and sea
had to be taken twice
could not be made one
without you there to see.

The trees all recede
in half-silhouette
float on softened mirrors
of eggshell and ash.

Where the sky should have been
everything diminishes
what needs to be carried
quietly into the fog
where we should be going.

The girl holds a stick
so loosely in her hand
light falls at her feet on leaves.

A moment gathers
in luminous folds
water and air
a speckled hill
her head to one side.

Her eyes beneath
a loose hat
overflow so quietly
down the bend of her stick
where light keeps falling
leaves appear
where everything given she
gives herself back to
makes the world breathe.

for Renata

Out here at the boundary
a path goes further
than anyone remembers
beyond things of wood and nails
even if they do remember
light in the overhead trees
the path divides.

Never having walked there
something unremembered
draws forward
past shacks of slats
and chimneys of tin
we would still follow.

As if everything could be
miniature halos of cloud
the warm earth releases
children come running
knee-deep in grass
and this makes them laugh.

There must be birds or cicadas
we can't hear in the brightness
waiting beyond this meadow
bound by memory to what must be
the mother and father
at the apex of a cape by a poplar
from a distance the laughter
only increases as the children run
and watching from here somehow
where the ground flattens
they come toward us.

for Max

So much depends now
on the stones.

Wind dies
but stones do not.

Some day this will make
all the difference
but not now.

Now we flower
and now we bend
disheveled.

A triangle of sky
beyond the promenade
balances on an unseen ocean
as wind roars from the sun
rips spectral colors from flags and dresses
sheds a trail of awnings and clouds
bleaches the holidays nameless.

Turning to face
the sea where it all comes from
recursive maps of dead languages
cataracts and rags of the empire
the ruins of orbits and numbers
all shimmer now in the searing light
rewrite these histories of the imagined
of words still unspoken of hope
of love not yet loved unsuspecting
its premonitions and eclipses
its sacraments of winches and clay and
pours in long hot sunlit streams
converging here above a hidden beach
out past a row of flimsy railings
on to the waiting continents.

for Wesley

What comes to be refused
itself refusing
a mass of headland
brightening some shelter.

Piers reflecting
things we can be sure of not
moving like shadows of sails.

All the pure touches
in air that just hangs there
as if it were made of nothing
but light and air.

No place
more precious
than another.

A shelter of trees
so lush and delicate
the defeated geometries
blow open softly
hold out their limbs to us
leaves as thin as birds' tongues
fill the air with green song
the multiplying sun
not a thing in the sky
but in beaches and grasses
its light still wet
on the lips of flowers
waving on long slender necks
pointing away from the water
half-covering the stones
a found place of ruins and hope
the wind overwhelms
with lobes and sprigs
and runners and wings.

for Anna

Untouched
portions of the plate
serve as a cramped sky
the smell of hunger
grown heavy with time
behind a kind of handle
whittled from a tree
the land inert
and of no color
the textures of grass
and stubble of ghosts
thick as horsehair.

Finally a path
would be wiped away
dug out with bare hands
staining the grooved
skin and metal and earth
down a merciless incline
from the sky
back to the body
again and again
scraped clean.

I've never been here before
but have seen the same sky
so many times
held at just this distance
the skin of a tree
smooth as a leg
where I would kneel
to press my mouth
the smell of damp lichen
still on my lips and face.

Everything my gaze
bathes and discards
falls to a bed of color
dissolves slowly enough
I remember in time
to trace and retrace
the braided light
smeared with lilac and pollen
smeared with nectar and dust
drawn forward and down
to a long imagined lake
cool as the underside of a new sheet
past grasses wet with shadows
the history of all the forgotten things
light drains from a weary horizon
to gather in fistfuls of peach and rose.

Let me wait a little longer
a wall of living shadows
flickering at the edge of a forest
cool and familiar.

Let me follow
the figures ahead
as slowly as a cloud.

Let me wrap
these bands of meadows
around a promised clearing
then wind them
on my head and arms
dress these damp wounds
secretly with their streamers
and dance out into the light.

Let the tears of the earth be
unafraid to stop
its dried blood
on my weathered hands
beaten to dust in golden air.

The Coach Road Landscapes are:

Ragpickers' Hut 1910 Eugène Atget
Seascape with Distant Coast 1845 J.M.W. Turner
Morning on the Banks of the Sèvre at Clisson 1884 François-Louis Français
Seacoast at Trouville 1881 Claude Monet
Twilight 1855-60 Jean-Baptiste-Camille Corot
Entrance to the Village of Osny 1881 Paul Gauguin
Rustic Building with Man under Trellis 1853   André Giroux
Pontoise, the Road to Gisors in Winter 1873 Camille Pissarro
The Seine At Chatou 1881   Pierre Auguste Renoir
The Bridge at Moret 1893   Alfred Sisley
Sunlight on the Road, Pontoise 1874 Camille Pisarro
Farmyard by Moonlight 1868   Jean-Francois Millet
Slave Ship (Slavers Throwing Overboard the Dead and Dying) 1840 J.M.W. Turner
Turn in the Road 1881 Paul Cézanne
Waves Breaking on a Lee Shore 1835 J.M.W. Turner
Roses under the Trees 1905 Gustave Klimt
The Pond 1877-79 Paul Cézanne
Storm Tide 1903   Robert Henri
Cloudy Sky - Mediterranean with Mount Agle 1859 Gustave LeGray
Lane in Fog, Arras 1860 Eugène Cuvelier
Young Girl with a Stick 1881 Camille Pissarro
Boundary of Barbizon 1860 Eugène Cuvelier
Path in the Long Grass 1875   Pierre-Auguste Renoir
Dandelions 1867-68   Jean-Francois Millet
Hotel des Roches Noirs, Trouville 1876 Claude Monet
Port-En-Bessin, Outer Harbor, High Tide 1888 Georges Seurat
The Path Up the Hill 1877-79 Edgar Dégas
Evening at Saint-Prive 1890 Henri-Joseph Harpignies
Meadow Bordered by Trees 1845 Pierre-Étienne-Théodore Rousseau

For links to images, visit fomitepress.com/cheap-gestures.htm

Fomite

Writing a review on social media sites for readers will help the progress of independent publishing. To submit a review, go to the book page on any of the sites and follow the links for reviews. Books from independent presses rely on reader-to-reader communications.

For more information or to order any of our books, visit:
fomitepress.com/our-books.html

More Odd Birds from Fomite...

William Benton
  Eye La View
Michael Breiner
  the way none of this happened
Roger Coleman
  The World Was Late
Bill Davis
  Cheap Gestures
Clare Dolan
  Museum of Everyday Life
J. C. Ellefson
  Under the Influence: Shouting Out to Walt
Stephen J. Goldberg
  Rants Raves & Ricochets
Joel Grossman
  Reading Embodied
David Ross Gunn
  Cautionary Chronicles
Andrei Guriuanu &Teknari
  Portraits of Time
  The Darkest City
Gail Holst-Warhaft
  The Fall of Athens
Sam Kerson
  Executions and Democracy

Fomite

   Gaza Punishing the Innocent
Michael Jewell
   The Memoirs of a Paper Doll
Daniil Kharms
   Connections (translator Roger Lebovitz, artist Delia Robinson)
Roger Lebovitz
   A Guide to the Western Slopes and the Outlying Area
   Blessings
   Twenty-two Instructions for Near Survival
Pippo Lionni
   Fat Facts of Life
dug Nap
   Artsy Fartsy
   Friends
Fletcher Oakes
   Modern Mandalas
Puppeteers
   Sourdough Rising
Delia Bell Robinson
   A Shirtwaist Story
   The Waters Prevail
Claire Russell
   Dear Mr. Thoreau
Clark Russrll
   Riddleville
Peter Schumann
   A Child's Deprimer
   Abrakadabra Yes No Apocalypse
   All
   All, Nothing, Nothing at All
   Bedsheet Mitigations
   Belligerent & Not So Belligerent Slogans from the Possibilitarian Arsenal
   Bread & Sentences
   Declaration of Light/Quo Vadis
   Diagonal Man Theory + Praxis, Volumes One and Two

Fomite

Erbarme dich – Have Mercy
Es is vollbracht - Mission Accomplished
Faust 3
Gaza Genocide Bedsheets
Handouts and Obligations
Kropotkin Speaks
Life and Death of Charlotte Salomon
Mister Aeschylus's The Persians
Planet Kasper, Volumes One and Two
Tears Clouds Trees
We
We Possibilitarians One and Two
Peter & Elka Schumann
  She Sits, She Rides, She Flies
Schütz, Heinrich
  Notes of Devastation
M.D. Uhser & T. Motley
  Poem A Mashup

www.ingramcontent.com/pod-product-compliance
Lightning Source LLC
Chambersburg PA
CBHW060515080526
44586CB00012B/495